STANDA

FOI

RACTICAL POETRY COURSE

Other Allison & Busby Writers' Guides

A PRACTICAL POETRY COURSE

Alison Chisholm

a&b

This edition published in Great Britain in 1997 by
Allison & Busby Ltd
114 New Cavendish Street
London W1M 7FD

First published in Great Britain in 1994 by Allison & Busby

A catalogue record for this book is available from
the British Library.

ISBN 0 74900 294 8

Typeset by TW Typesetting, Plymouth, Devon
Printed and bound in Great Britain by
Mackays of Chatham plc, Chatham, Kent

A PRACTICAL POETRY COURSE

INTRODUCTION

If you are interested in writing poetry, this practical course is for you. You may be a novice where writing is concerned, and will want to cover basic aspects of the craft. If you are an experienced practitioner, you will have an opportunity to flex the writing muscle and to broaden your spheres of interest.

The course consists of eleven schedules. You will gain the greatest benefit from these if you are able to allow yourself a 'poetry day' for the completion of each one. Do not worry if your lifestyle will not permit you the luxury of a full day in which to write. Dip into the book and tackle just one or two of the exercises. If you wish, attempt each section at a different time. Although some schedules offer complementary ideas, each area of the schedule can stand on its own, in isolation from the others. The schedules may be used over and over again. They approach the craft and practice of poetry from six directions. These are:

READING	An exploration of contemporary and classical poetry, one of the most useful exercises for any poet.
WRITING	Practical experience of putting words on to paper.
ADMINISTRATION	Handling the business side of writing.
FUN	The essential relaxation in the craft.
FORM	A study of new and traditional forms of poetry.
WORKSHOP	The development and moulding of your poems, and writing exercises.

1

Initially the only requirements for the course are pen and paper, a notebook and collections of poetry. In order to complete the Administration aspects of each schedule you will need a little more stationery and access to a typewriter/word processor. The Reading areas require books which many poets will already have. With the possible exception of poetry magazines, all publications will be available in the library – but you may consider it wise to buy these books for future reference.

If the idea of working in this way seems too clinical or does not appeal to you, remember that the course is not designed to sap the artistry of your writing. The best poems will still be those which burn into your mind and force you to set them down. The task of putting their words on to paper will be made easier if writing poetry is a delicious habit for you rather than a rare and strange event.

You will note that many of the exercises offered should produce publishable work, or even poetry of competition standard. Remember that the exercises are designed to produce first drafts. They will probably need revision before making the grade.

You may be happier working by yourself, or with a friend or group of poets. (The Administration part of the schedule is the only area in which it is easier to work alone.) Whether alone or in company, it is a good idea to work your way through this book rather than merely read it from cover to cover. Take a day at a time, and ideally allow yourself a break of at least a week before attempting the next day's schedule. During the week use your spare time to increase your experience of all aspects of your last poetry day.

The one problem with following the course by yourself is that it is hard to assess the value of the work you are producing and the improvements in your poetry. If you can share your work with a group or class, well and good. If you cannot, practise standing back from your own work and evaluating it ruthlessly. But do not attempt to do this until some time has elapsed since you wrote the piece in question.

If you start working through any exercise and your imagination or inspiration prompts you to abandon it and write something else, follow your instinct. The exercise will still be there for a day when your creative juices are not flowing.

Remember that creating poetry, however enjoyable, is demanding and tiring work. It is good to be disciplined in your writing projects, but do not stretch yourself to a point where writing becomes a chore. Know your limitations, and stop for a break or abandon the schedule altogether if your pleasure or sense of involvement in the craft begins to diminish.

As you approach each poetry day, create a convenient timetable for your work. My preference is to spend 30–45 minutes on each exercise, and to break for coffee, a meal or a walk after two exercises. Experiment to discover your own most enjoyable and effective manner of working. Then use the blueprint of the schedule to create your own additional writing days pursuing your special interests in poetry.

Happy writing.

DAY ONE

Reading

The more poetry you read, the better will be the poetry you write. A careful analysis of your reading is an extremely valuable aid to your own writing. Read from the latest copy of any poetry magazine. Start by reading purely for pleasure, flicking through the pages and taking poems at random. Read silently and aloud, and ask yourself whether the sound of the words adds to your comprehension of the poem, or whether you find it distracting.

Allow yourself to absorb the sheer joy of poetry for a while. Then start to study the magazine in greater depth. Do any themes or styles predominate? Is each poet represented by a single piece, or by a number of poems? Are the poets' names familiar to you? Do 'unknowns' feature alongside big names? Does the magazine favour long or short poems? Does any title intrigue you? Which poem appeals to you most strongly? Can you say why it appeals, or are you responding to gut reaction?

Make a note of the pieces you find most effective, whether or not you like them. Put the magazine down for a few minutes. Which poems remain freshest in your memory?

These are considerations from the reader's point of view. Now look at your list of the most effective poems through the eyes of a writer.

For each, ask yourself what prompted the poet to introduce that particular poem. Does it share a message or emotion? Does it deal with heavy, concentrated subject matter or trivia? Does it make its point forcefully or subtly? Do you think it was throbbing inside its creator, commanding him to put it on paper? Or, in your opinion, was he toying with the pen when he simply decided to jot down a few lines? (For the sake of convenience I refer to the poet as 'he' throughout, but this invariably implies 'he or she'.)

Is there anything about the title, form or style of the poem which draws your attention? Is the use of metaphor and imagery predictable, or does it surprise you? Does the poem seem fresh and original, or have you heard it all before? If there is originality, is it in the area of subject matter or of the poet's treatment of his material? Are there words and phrases which will stick in your memory? Are there any techniques or devices of poetry that surprise (or shock) and delight you?

Make notes of all these observations. Not only will they help to fix a memorable poem still more firmly in your mind. They will also, by example, add to your store of knowledge of the craft of writing.

You have considered the magazine as a reader and a writer. With or without realising it, you have also analysed it as a potential contributor. Look at any editorial matter included. Couple the information you glean there with your opening comments about the make-up of the magazine, and you have completed some useful market study.

Writing

Begin by steeping yourself in contemporary poetry. Read in order to tune yourself into the rhythms and patterns that will underpin your own writing. When you are bursting to write, start setting down words on paper.

At this stage, it does not matter what you are writing. The important thing is to let your words flow, to let them pour out in whatever form they care to take. Write quickly, without allowing yourself to think. Start with the first words that come into your head. If nothing comes, start with the last line of the poem you have just read. Then keep writing, making sense if you can, producing rubbish if you cannot.

The only discipline you should impose on yourself is to try to write in separate lines rather than as a continuous piece. Then when you stop writing (after about five minutes), the work you have produced will have the shape of a poem rather than of a piece of prose.

It is highly unlikely that your words will form a poem. But you will have warmed up the 'writing muscle', putting yourself into a frame of mind from which the poetry may flow.

Do not abandon these outpourings altogether. Put them on one side and re-read them later. While you were avoiding conscious thought, your subconscious might have started to guide you along a route which is worth pursuing.

Having warmed up to writing, let yourself continue to pour words on to paper, but approach the words with a little more discipline. The aim now is to produce a good volume of material, but it should be in first draft form rather than totally unformed. In other words, keep reading over to yourself the words you are producing. Build up a pattern of lines and stanzas, following your thoughts and ideas to a conclusion. Be aware of the need to have something to say, and your inherent desire to communicate through your poetry.

For subject matter, draw on the concerns which have surrounded your life in recent days. Write about any feeling or reaction you have experienced that you wish to share with others. Look at the material making up the poetry in which you steeped yourself for this exercise. Do you have a personal viewpoint to express on one of these themes? Is an idea – maybe on a quite different subject – sparked off by something you have read?

When your flow of ideas begins to subside, or when you find your mind wandering far from the poetry you are beginning to create, stop writing. The energy of your poems will be sapped if you are becoming tired or bored.

Remember that a short attention span at this time does not indicate a low boredom threshold. It is a natural response to the high level of concentration writing poetry demands.

7

By now you should have produced the 'nonsense' outpourings of the beginning of the session, and one or several poems in very rough form, possibly no more than notes. Put these aside for consideration later in the day, or at some future date. You have achieved something useful. It is a lot easier to take an unprepossessing draft and craft it into a poem than to produce that draft in the first place.

Administration

Spend half an hour working on your poetry notes. It is a good idea to use a small notebook rather than a file or exercise book, as it is worth being able to carry this around with you.

Write down words or phrases which you find pleasing, whether you have heard them spoken aloud or they have simply popped into your head.

Store observations you have made about both the inconsequential and the earth shattering events of everyday life.

Record any original similes or metaphors that occur to you.

Note down your dreams and daydreams, your fantasies. If hearing a tale makes you think to yourself 'but what if such-and-such happened?' supply conclusions from your imagination.

Put into words the feelings that rage within you, revelling in the positive ones and finding catharsis in recording the negative.

Make a note of any circumstances which prompted you to think they might be worth exploring in writing. Make fuller notes of anything which made you think 'I must write a poem about that'.

Jot down any potential titles for poems which come into your head, remembering that a challenging or intriguing title may help to sell a poem or to gain recognition for it in a competition.

In all your notes write carefully observed details rather than generalities. Poetry which focuses on detailed realities is stronger than that which waffles in abstractions.

For your own convenience, it is useful to store all of these observations in your notebook rather than among a clutter of used envelopes and shopping-lists. You will, however, have your own ideas about the degree of order in your notebook.

If you have an organised mind and think clearly in lists, keep separate areas of your book with headings such as 'titles' and 'dreams'. If you are happy with chaos, jumble together all your ideas. This is a small point, but a valid one. To provide you with the maximum of stimulus, your notes should reflect your own most comfortable way of working.

You may find that you refer to your notebook frequently, drawing random ideas from it or working methodically from cover to cover. Even when you have worked each of its ideas, retain the book – never throw it away. A single point which inspired you to write one poem may, at a later date, be the inspiration for a dozen more.

At the other extreme, you may find that you write continually in your notebook and yet never draw anything from it. Carrying the book around with you is still beneficial. After all, the day may come when you believe there is nothing in the world about which you want to write, and yet you burn with the poet's desire to produce something. Your notebook could present a solution. Even if you never look back at the words you have written, the notebook has provided a useful dumping ground for the observations and ideas you needed to get out of your system.

Fun

For total relaxation from the heavier tasks of writing poetry, create a few lines of personal poetry for sheer amusement.

Think of the next occasion when a friend or relative will be celebrating, and write a lighthearted poem in honour of the event. People who do not write poetry themselves are normally delighted to have a piece specially written for them, with messages and references only they (and perhaps their friends) can understand.

The style of your poem will depend on the nature of the event and how well you know the person concerned. For example, you may write a humorous verse for a friend's 'milestone' birthday, or something more sentimental for an elderly couple's wedding anniversary.

Keep your tone light and, unless your piece is dedicated to another poet, use a traditional form with rhyme and rhythm for popular appeal. Make sure that you stay with your chosen rhyming and rhythmic pattern for the greatest effect.

It may be appropriate to write something abusive or risqué for a particular event, but let your own good taste impose limitations. You want to add to the celebration, not cause distress and embarrassment to the subject of your poem, or to any friends who may hear it.

Personal poetry is not restricted to adults. You can delight a young child by writing the simplest of poems about him, particularly if his toys, pets or brothers and sisters are mentioned. A story devised especially for the child and written in rhyme is likely to become a favourite, and because of the verse structure will be memorable. The recipient will be able to quote from it long after you have forgotten writing it.

Whether for a child or an adult, your poem should be one which can be read aloud for everyone's amusement; but do make sure that your subject receives a copy to keep as a memento of the occasion.

Form

The Minute is a very short poem, challenging and fun to write. It was originated by Verna Lee Hinegardner of Arkansas. It consists of 60 syllables divided into 12 lines. The metre is iambic, i.e., divided into feet of two syllables, the first being unstressed and the second stressed.

The first, fifth and ninth lines have eight syllables (four feet) each. All the other lines have four syllables (two feet).

Rhymes occur in couplets, so the first two lines rhyme together, lines three and four rhyme etc. The pattern of the poem, counting the first rhyming sound as 'a', the second as 'b' and so on is:

a a b b c c d d e e f f

Other requirements of the form are that it should be punctuated as prose and have capital letters at the beginning of a new sentence rather than at the start of each line. The essence of the minute is that it should represent a momentary mood or a minute in time.

Example: *Insomnia*

When darkness drapes a wakeful night	a
and grants you sight	a
to stroll or zoom	b
about my room	b
in fragmentary memories,	c
I grasp to seize	c
the best of you	d
that filters through	d
my midnight melancholy skies.	e
And when my eyes	e
no longer weep,	f
I fall asleep.	f

Verna Lee Hinegardner

This form does not lend itself easily to communicating weighty ideas or propounding philosophies. It is a vehicle for cameo thoughts, whimsical fancies. Nevertheless the challenge of short lines, tight rhymes, controlled metre and carefully selected subject matter make it an intriguing form in which to write.

Workshop

Originality is the aim of every poet, and extremely difficult to attain. It is worth spending an occasional half-hour devoting yourself to the pursuit of innovation.

The only way you can be 100 percent inventive in poetry is by dreaming up a subject which has never been addressed before, and by exploring it in vocabulary you have devised, in a form you have discovered. Perhaps if you achieved true originality, it would be totally incomprehensible to the rest of the world. In that case your poem would have failed as a form of communication, and a poem which does not communicate in any way has little to commend it.

In seeking originality, it is better to search for your own voice than to aim for a piece of writing which is unique in every aspect. Remind yourself that even the most tried themes have something new to offer when filtered through your particular perceptions.

While thinking around a theme, try to forget what everybody else has said about it. This is more difficult than it sounds. Ask yourself, as a child would ask, 'What does this look like or feel like to me?'

Answer with simplicity and honesty. There is a better chance that you will come up with a new idea in total sincerity than by trying to impose sophisticated thoughts on to your assessment.

You can use anything as a starting point. For example, the sight of a green field may remind you of an exercise book, a garment of the same colour, a flag. Resist the temptation to think of verdant rolling meadows or a viridescent swell. They have been used before.

Make a further exploration of your individual assessment. Using the same example, the field may remind you of a flag.

The rippling of grass has a parallel with the fluttering of the flag in a breeze. The flag itself might remind you of childhood visits to the seaside, and those paper flags you used to stick into sand castles. It is now a very short step from your original field to a whole network of images which are highly personal to you, and so place the field firmly in the area of your individual voice.

Spend a little time noting down not only the images connected with your starting point, but also words and phrases, similes and metaphors which surround the subject for you. When you have exhausted your fresh ideas, go back to the clichés which abound on your subject. See whether you can twist them into a new and thought-provoking form. Staying with the field, you have studiously ignored 'verdant rolling meadows'. Twist this into 'green-rolled meadows' and you have a new phrase with an associated image of house painting.

Delve into your subject until you have discovered all its depths, and see whether there is a poem crying out to be written. If there is, write it. If there is not, keep all your notes on file. You will be able to use them at some stage.

Exercises

1   Think of the emotion you experienced most recently. Try to put your precise feelings into words. Liken the emotion to an animal, and suggest vocabulary which would link the two.
2   Recall an incident from your childhood. Was it a common experience, one with which many people could identify, or something few would share? Make notes about it, remembering as many details as possible.
3   Write down six sayings or clichés. Now for each of them think of original ways to express the same idea.

DAY TWO

Reading

Have a look at a collection of poetry from the past. Concentrate either on Shakespeare's sonnets or on the poetry of the First World War.

If you have chosen the sonnets, think first about the length of time which has passed since they were written. These poems have a classical, even ancient 'feel' about them, but their message is universal. Although today's lover would express himself in different terms, the emotions he experiences and reactions to his beloved are the same as those described centuries ago.

Allow the beauty of the language to flow over you for a few moments. Do not worry about identifying obscure allusions or analysing convoluted phrases. Open your mind to the richness of the words, and the delights of luxuriating in them.

Now think a little more closely about the vocabulary used and the precise meaning of each line. Note the balance between plain, simple words and more flowery expressions. Some poets might find it useful to write a prose draft of a sonnet in contemporary language; for others, that would kill the magic inherent in the poem. Try doing this if you feel it will help you towards a better understanding.

Consider the quantity of material in the sonnet. Is it appropriate for the tight length of fourteen lines? Would you like to read more, or do you think the point could be put across in fewer words? Is the balance of the sonnet correctly maintained? Does the final couplet open any new windows in your mind or offer a satisfying conclusion? Make your judgments honestly, without allowing yourself to be intimidated by the enormity of the poet's stature. You are reading as a fellow craftsman, not as a disciple.

If you have chosen the war poetry, it might be useful to begin by reflecting on the age that produced the poems. You do not need to be an historian. You will be able to remind yourself of the historical background by referring to an encyclopaedia, or simply by recalling all that you have seen, heard or read about the period 1914–18.

Try to imagine the circumstances in which the poems you are reading were produced. Can you see the despair of the soldier in the trenches, surrounded by death and destruction? Are you seeing through the eyes of an officer or one of the men? Are you looking on the scene with a dispassionate view, distanced by time or space from the events of the war? Are the poems full of jingoism or pity? Can you identify with them, or do they seem remote and unreal?

Ask yourself how the poet created the effects to which you are reacting. In technical terms, did he use rhyme and metre or a pattern of free verse to paint his picture? Is his use of language controlled or chaotic? Is the vocabulary flowing or staccato?

Artistically, does he focus your attention on a wide panorama or on a tiny detail? Does he let you make your own judgments or tell you what to think? Does he impose his emotions on you, or allow your own to leap to a spontaneous response?

Compare the poetry of this period with your knowledge of other times of war, from distant history to the present day. Do the years 1914–18 reflect common reactions, or were they unique? Which of the wars of history is the most vivid in your imagination? Can you discover poems written about it?

Whichever set of work you studied, you were looking at one of the universal and timeless subjects for writing poetry. The deeper your understanding of poems of the past, the more likely you are to create living poems in today's voice on such subjects.

Writing

Create your own love or war poem. Write it in any form, perhaps imitating the pattern (although not, of course, the vocabulary or ideas) of one of the poems you have just read.

Remember that you are dealing with a topic which could have a profound effect on your readers. Somebody who is celebrating the joys of discovering love will be pleased to recognise your understanding of the feelings involved. Your writing will be most poignant for any reader who has just come through a difficult romantic experience, or who has known bereavement or suffering through war.

You owe it to these readers, as well as to yourself, to write with complete sincerity. This does not mean that you must have experienced at first hand the circumstances which provide your subject matter. You must have thought about them deeply, though, and speak out the truth as you understand it. Your interpretation of the experiences of others is valid and honest, as long as you strive to offer it with sincerity.

You are looking at two of the most frequently used subjects for poetry. Before you begin to write, search your imagination for new insights into your well-worn topic, or for an angle of approach which is unusual and telling.

Decide on a suitable focus for your poem. A poem about 'love' would be vague and full of words illustrating abstractions. A poem concerning the precise feelings of a lover on discovering that a partner has been unfaithful, focuses with greater strength.

Do not yield to the temptation of making global points in your poem, particularly when you have concentrated on a careful directing of its focus. A poem describing the effects of a land mine loses its significance if it deteriorates into a diatribe against war in general.

Throughout the writing process, be especially aware of the words and phrases which are always to be found within your range of subject matter. Look around you for original descriptions which will startle with their precision. Look inside yourself to examine your own emotions, and write exactly what you feel, uninfluenced by other people's thoughts.

It will always save you heartache and discomfiture if you put the finished first draft of your poem away for a period of time before submitting it for publication. (The length of time varies for the individual poet and also for the individual poem.) This is especially important in the case of a poem on an emotive subject.

The strength of your feelings about the subject of your poem could cloud your judgment regarding its technical merits. Pull the critic's hat down firmly over your ears before you begin your analysis. Allow yourself a greater distance of time than usual between creation and submission. But do not forget that an air of spontaneity will make your poem breathe with life. Iron it into creases which are too measured, and it will be stifled.

The balance between revised and spontaneous writing has no rules to govern its application. You have to trust to your poetic instinct, remembering that your instinct develops – and becomes more reliable – as you progress.

Administration

Check out the degree of organisation to be found in the copies of your work. You may have neatly typed and numbered copies of revision stages of every piece you have written. If such is the case, omit this part of your poetry day, and spend the time saved working on the other half of the 'writing' section. Write a love poem if you had previously produced a war poem, and vice versa.

If your work is not in such tidy order, spend some time producing good copies. These must be typed and, although the effect of using a sophisticated word processor may be the most attractive, copies produced by an ordinary manual typewriter are acceptable.

Check through your notebooks and – especially – any scraps of paper on which you might have written poems. Make your typed copies of the best version of each poem before you run the risk of mislaying it. Your best version may, of course, be its most recent revision or an earlier attempt.

Do not throw out your handwritten drafts. You never know when you will want to return to them in order to extract some material you require for a different poem. You may realise that your 'best' version of a poem does not work quite as well as you expected it to, and wish to go back to an earlier draft. If you have disposed of your drafts, you will have lost the access to your poem's development. You will also find that the lost portions acquire enhanced status in your mind simply because they are unattainable. You will waste time and creative energy agonising over their disappearance.

Having made neat copies, store them away using some method which will allow you to retrieve them easily. You may keep them in chronological order of writing. You may prefer to keep an alphabetical listing of titles or of first lines. If you use this method, be sure to keep a note of titles you may have changed. (I once suffered the embarrassment of sending the same poem to two magazines simultaneously under two different titles.)

It is a good idea to keep paper copies of all poems even when you are using a word processor. Accidents can happen, and a corrupted disc can wipe out ten years' work. If the unthinkable should occur, the chore of retyping a few hundred poems is infinitely preferable to losing all trace of them.

When making your typed copies, prepare them in the standard format for submission to a poetry editor. When they are presented in this fashion, you will have a good idea of how they would look in print. Type each, however short, on its own sheet of A4-size paper. Leave sufficient space for top and left-hand margins so that the poem does nct appear to be cramped in a corner. It is in order to use the single-space setting on your typewriter or printer when submitting poetry, rather than the double-spaced presentation required for other pieces of writing.

Be accurate. If you cannot type, learn to do so. If you type badly, practise. A poem showing poor presentation implies that its writer was not sufficiently interested in it to concentrate on the detail of its appearance. Remember that correction fluid hides a multitude of sins – and can remain a secret if you get good quality photocopies made of your poetry. (The copies do not show the crusty white evidence of dried correction fluid.)

Once you have made pleasing copies of your work, read and enjoy them. There is nothing wrong with looking back over your writing. It will help to prompt further ideas for pieces you will produce in the future. It may show up flaws you had not noticed before. It should certainly enhance your confidence in your writing.

Fun

If writing poetry is important to you, you will approach your craft in a serious frame of mind. An occasional lightening of your mood will often enhance the rest of your writing.

The whole business of poetry can be taken too seriously. Experiment by exploring poets and their work through lighthearted prose. You may not produce writing of great artistic or literary merit, and commercial success is not guaranteed, but you will have relaxed and loosened the metaphorical belt a notch or two, and that is always to be recommended.

Try writing a short story about a poet visiting a school, and being confronted by the most unsavoury group of nine-year-olds imaginable. Or write a monologue from the viewpoint of a bored housewife who finds solace in her 'double life' as a poet. Write a fictional account of some unusual occurrence within a poetry group, or let your mind carry a set of characters into some time in the future, when the skill of writing a poem is a highly desirable achievement.

Impose your imagination on to poets of the past. Write the script for a first meeting between Wordsworth and Coleridge.

20

Produce fictional diary entries for Byron during his time in Venice. Construct the letters Elizabeth Barrett Browning might have written home from Italy.

These are just a few sketchy ideas. You will be able to supply plenty more, and your self-imposed tasks will have the added spice of characters and situations of your own choosing.

This is a frivolous exercise, and may seem a little too silly for comfort, but there are three major benefits to be gained from it.

First, you are writing about poetry – something you acknowledge to be important in your life. Any material you produce within this subject area should automatically appeal to you. The more it appeals, the better the results will be.

Secondly, for the purposes of this exercise, you are writing in prose. Practising any style of writing is good for your handling of other styles. You will return to your poetry refreshed from this foray into fictional prose.

Finally it is always possible that you might produce a commercially acceptable short story from the initial set of ideas, or a monologue to be delivered in public. Every acceptance brings a boost to your confidence, essential for all writers, regardless of their degree of experience – and you may even earn some cash for your labours.

Form

The Italian Quatrain is a stanza made up of four lines of iambic pentameter (i.e. five feet to a line, each consisting of an unstressed syllable followed by a stressed one). The first and last lines rhyme, and the second and third lines rhyme, creating the pattern.

a b b a

As this is the form of individual stanzas, any number of quatrains can be used to create a poem. Subsequent stanzas take their own rhyming sounds, so the rhyme plan for a poem of four stanzas would be:

a b b a   c d d c   e f f e   g h h g

The pattern is attractive, easy to follow and versatile. Its sound effect is a little more subtle than that of a quatrain which rhymes alternate lines.

Example: *Neapolitan Fisherman*

His voice rose when his boat was just a speck	a
That bobbed on waves of sound across the bay.	b
I could not see the singer, for he lay	b
Spreadeagled on the salted, net-strewn deck.	a
He recognised no music, sang no scores;	c
Confused arpeggios surged from his throat,	d
Excess of pleasure hurling every note	d
To echo back from far volcanic shores.	c
As he drew close, he stood and waved a hand,	e
Called out a careless greeting. I replied	f
By waving in my turn from high cliffside,	f
And watched him drag his boat up gravelled sand.	e
I looked again; saw only brine and foam.	g
But when Italian tenors soar in song	h
The moment comes alive, and I belong	h
To distant lands a world away from home.	g

If the subject of your poem suggests that you use a quatrain form, it is interesting to experiment with a number of different patterns to see which is the most effective.

Workshop

Analysing a poem in detail is unlikely to be the best way of appreciating it. As a writer of poetry, you should be aware of the devices used by other poets, and of their relative effectiveness. Apply this analysis checklist to any poem which speaks clearly to you, whether you like the poem or not. Make notes of your answers, and give them some thought. If you can discover how a poem works, you will be able to apply its techniques to your own poetry. You will be creating a do-it-yourself masterclass.

Poetry Analysis Checklist

1 Do you like the poem? Why – or why not?
2 What is its theme?
3 Is the theme well communicated?
4 What is its subject matter?
5 Is subject matter appropriate to the theme?
6 Is enough subject material included? Is there too much or too little?
7 What do you think of the title? Is it memorable?
8 Is the poem written in any set pattern? How is the pattern handled?
9 Is the pattern of the poem on the page appropriate?
10 Are stanza divisions (if any) appropriate?
11 Is the tone of the poem pleasing?
12 Is there effective use of imagery?
13 Is the vocabulary well selected?
14 Is line/sentence construction appropriate?
15 Does the punctuation – or lack of it – work?
16 Is there rhyme? If so, is it regular? Do deviations from rhyme add to or detract from the effect of the poem?
17 Is there a metrical pattern? If so, is it regular? Do deviations from it add to or detract from the effect?
18 Are literary devices and/or eccentricities (e.g. invented grammar or vocabulary) used to good effect?

19 If other work by the same poet is known:
(a) Is it as good as/better than/worse than you would expect from this poet?
(b) How does this piece fit into the overall spectrum of the poet's output?
(c) Does the poem 'feel' right? Was the poet comfortable with this form, theme etc.?

20 How does the poem fit in with your personal definitions of poetry? E.g.:
(a) Is the poem memorable?
(b) Are the best words used in the best order? Or the only words in the only order?
(c) Does the poem communicate something from its writer to its reader? (The reader may, of course, be the same person.)
(d) Is the poet making sense of the world around him, and the world within him?

Although this checklist is designed for use with the poetry of other people, applying it to your own poem can sometimes help to clarify your feelings about a problem area within the poem.

Exercises

1   Set yourself a list of words with obvious connections between them, then add a 'cuckoo' word, which does not belong with the rest. E.g. you might choose flame, ember, heat, flicker, amber ... and clock. Produce a poem in any style which uses all of the words.
2   Play about with tercets – stanzas of three lines. Experiment with different line lengths, with a strict or haphazard beat, and with all permutations of the use of rhyme. Expand any stanza pattern which pleases you into a complete poem.
3   Explore the mythology and folklore of any natural thing

– flower, animal, ore, etc. Make notes of your findings for use as either a passing reference or the main subject of a poem.

DAY THREE

Reading

Explore a new dimension in poetry by reading some work which has foreign connections.

It may have been originated in your own tongue, but in a different country. How does it differ from a poem on a similar subject from your own land? Do you find the same themes recurring, or is a wealth of unexpected material on offer? Is the handling of subject matter more direct or oblique than you might have expected? If you did not know its origins, would you realise that it was not 'home grown'?

Do any particular forms predominate? Are most of the poems strictly patterned, or is free verse favoured? Do you discover any forms which are new to you?

Because of the singular quality of every poem written, it is difficult to draw general conclusions. Read as much as you can to give yourself an overview of your selected country's poetry.

Your chosen poetry may have been written in another language. If you are able to read and understand it in its original form, well and good. If you have a smattering of the language but not full comprehension, it is still worth studying the work in the original. You will be able to grasp some of the essential flavour of the writing, and by reading it aloud, even with only slight knowledge of its language, you will be able to appreciate its cadences, and the sound it creates.

If you have no understanding at all, enjoy the poems in translation. Ask yourself the questions suggested above.

Then analyse what must be your subjective view of the translator's work. Is the translation fluent or stilted? Is the vocabulary precise? Has the idiom of the language been captured? Has the translator managed to incorporate poetic devices, such as rhyme, alliteration, puns or metre?

If at all possible, read translations of your chosen poetry by two or more different people. Which appeals to you most strongly? Where do the translations diverge?

Perhaps you have selected poems written in your own language by somebody whose native tongue is not yours. Does anything about them seem awkward? Or do they move with a natural flow? Does the subject matter touch on the country of its writer's birth, maybe on cultures and landscapes which are alien to you?

As you read, are you aware of any struggle to produce language in its most heightened form, or do you instantly forget that the poet was not born and bred on your doorstep?

Compare, if you can, a poem by your chosen writer with one on a similar theme by a writer using his first language. Are any interesting insights revealed? This exercise is very useful as a means of analysing language.

The obvious advantages of reading work with a foreign connection are the extending of your knowledge of another culture, and an exploration of the poetic diction and style of that culture.

At the end of your reading period, ask yourself whether you have learned anything new, and be honest about your answer. If the answer is no – no matter – you have broadened your knowledge of poetry, the most valuable aid to your own writing. If the answer is yes, you have added to the store of experience on which you draw every time you put pen to paper.

Writing

If you have knowledge of a foreign language, why not try your hand at translation? This suggestion is made purely for your own enjoyment. Professional translating is a skill of the highest order, and colloquial use of both languages is essential. But you can amuse yourself and deepen your insights into the poetry of other cultures by dabbling, even if your abilities extend little further than 'la plume de ma tante'. As an added bonus, you will also extend your language skills.

The exercise is a good lesson in poetic construction, and makes you consider all the alternative ways of phrasing an idea rather than merely jotting down your first thought.

It is fascinating to attempt to translate a poem, and afterwards to read a professional translation of the same piece. Compare the two versions carefully, not just to check for errors, but to look at the choice of language and idiom in each example.

Consider ideas for a poem which reaches beyond your immediate vicinity to foreign countries you know, or which are in the news, or which you may simply have thought about recently.

Having decided on a location, you need to plan how crucial the influence of place is to be within the poem you wish to write. For example, you may want to write a poem about a relationship, and it is a matter of slight interest that the background happens to be another country. On the other hand, you may want to write a poem about a foreign landmark such as the Eiffel Tower, the topography of a place, or a fact which is inextricably linked with a geographical identity, such as the Boston Tea Party.

As you make notes for your poem, remember to check any details you intend to quote about a place. If you guess at a fact, you can guarantee that the first person who looks at your poem knows all the true facts. A hint of inaccuracy in your writing carries ripples of uncertainty through the reader. If the details are wrong, the poem is devalued.

Beware of writing a travelogue, a poem which simply describes a place in guide-book fashion and has nothing else to offer. It might make an attractive cameo piece to interest somebody who knows the area, but will have little to offer the general reader.

If you are determined to write a purely descriptive poem, be sure to highlight details rather than giving an overall impression. In this style of poem remember, too, that your use of vocabulary must be precise. Words like 'beautiful', 'stunning' and 'spectacular' are the clichés of scenic descriptions. Work to produce more interesting and challenging adjectives.

However strongly your location features in your poem, be sure to avoid giving the reader a geography lesson. Only put down those points which are essential to full comprehension of the message you are trying to communicate. A reader with knowledge of your location will supply his own mental pictures. One with no such knowledge will use – and enjoy using – his imagination.

Where it is skilfully woven into the text of your poem, an appropriate location gives colour and depth. Mishandle it, and you weaken your writing.

Administration

It is useful to organise the copies of your poetry into a number of categories. A category filing system is valuable both for ease of finding copies of your work and for helping yourself in the business of assessment and appreciation of your writing.

The way you choose to categorise your work is a highly individual decision, but, however you do it, you are making yourself think carefully about the poetry you have produced.

You may wish to keep together material covering certain areas of subject matter, giving you immediate access to your full range of poems on a particular subject, and a clear view of the angles you have covered on that theme.

If you find writing in set forms stimulating, it may be helpful to keep all the strict form work, free verse, syllabic poetry, etc. in separate areas.

A more difficult (but perhaps more helpful) division is based on your honest appraisal of the potential of your poems. You may split them by selecting the very best for submission to competitions, the good ones to send to magazines, and those which do not quite work to your satisfaction for further attention.

Your categories may be for the poems you wish to share with a wider audience or for those personal pieces you wish to keep to yourself or to show to close friends.

The practice of categorising poems is a useful habit to cultivate regardless of the number of pieces you have written. The novice poet may feel that half-a-dozen poems do not merit such selection, but, even at this early stage, it helps to judge each poem in the context of the entire output.

Devise the system of categories which is most helpful to your way of working, and then make sure that you file away your poems in the appropriate areas at regular intervals. By doing this, you will save valuable time. Finding your way around your own work becomes a much simpler operation, and keeps copies of your best poetry instantly available for submission.

Fun

Part of the joy of writing poetry is the sheer pleasure to be gained from manipulating the language. Playing with words and exploring the best way to convey a message in a very few words will help you to attune this manipulation more finely.

One of the shortest, tightest forms of writing is the slogan. Advertisers know the power of a memorable, snappy phrase which can become synonymous with a product. Poets can do a lot worse than spend a few minutes of their spare time trying to think up similarly clever phrases to describe absolutely anything.

The most useful application of this practice is the production of slogans for competitions. Many trade competitions require entrants to perform a simple task, perhaps answering easy questions or identifying the differences between two almost identical pictures. Having performed this task, the competitor has to complete a tie-breaker in the form of a slogan, often relating to the sponsor's product.

Read the requirements carefully. There is usually a special angle to contemplate. For example, you may be asked to complete a sentence in the most witty or appropriate fashion. You may be asked to give reasons for selecting the product, or list its most appealing features.

Think of all the devices poets use to make their work memorable. Is there scope to use rhyme, a strong beat, alliteration or a pun? Can you create a tongue-twister or a joke around the product?

Whatever technique you use, make sure that you satisfy the requirements of the competition. If your slogan is to have a maximum of fifteen words, the most brilliant entry in the competition cannot be considered if it contains 16.

There may be part of a sentence which you have to complete. If the competition is run by, for example, Penelope's Pizza Company, you might have to respond to:

I choose Penelope's Pizzas because ...

or

Penelope's Pizzas are popular because ...

or

More pizza-lovers love Penelope's Pizzas because ...

Each wording seems to be looking for a slightly different response, obviously in praise of the product. As a poet you are accustomed to analysing and questioning every word.

In the first example, you will note the use of 'I'. This implies a personal comment. The word 'choose' connected with pizza suggests a range of flavours. So an appropriate end to the sentence might incorporate your own taste coupled with the breadth of choice available.

The second example does not refer to a person, but concentrates on a product. The alliteration in the company name added to the use of the word 'popular' might lead you to conclude the sentence by bringing in more words beginning with 'p' in praise of the pizzas.

The third example highlights alliteration and uses repetition. Characters are introduced once again, and the presence of 'love' and 'lovers' hints at a lighthearted romantic angle. Suggestions of togetherness in sharing a pizza, marriage of flavours, couples, etc. might be appropriate.

This form of analysis can only provide you with hints. There is no guarantee that it will work, but it might give you a better chance than merely jotting down the first words that come into your head. They will probably be the first words that come into everybody else's head, too. Above all, you want your entry to stand out from the crowd, and to stay in the judge's memory.

The real value in the practice of writing slogans lies in the attention focused on to a tiny phrase, and your skill in creating a slogan from the most telling words in the most exciting format. As a secondary consideration, there is always the chance that yours will be the winning competition tie-breaker and earn you a prize. Good luck!

Form

Sapphic quatrains, which take their name from the Greek poet Sappho, are unrhymed and rely on a harmony of metrical pattern to work as a poetic form. The stanzas comprise units of construction. Any number of the quatrains can be used to create your poem.

The first three lines of each stanza have an identical pattern of two trochees, a dactyl and another two trochees. The fourth line is shorter, consisting of one dactyl and a trochee.

The trochee has the reverse pattern of an iambus, i.e. it consists of a stressed syllable followed by an unstressed one. The dactyl is a foot of three syllables, one stressed followed by two unstressed.

Where / indicates a stressed and x an unstressed syllable, an example of the full line's metre would be:

```
 /   x / x  /  x   x  /  x   /  x
Wide piazza shimmers, and tree-fringed pathways
```

33

while the shorter, final line's pattern would be:

     / × × /   ×

    Glint in a heat haze.

The fourth line is frequently indented by a couple of spaces when sapphics are typed, but this is a matter of choice.

Example: *A Night with Figaro*

    Lighting dims as overture's first notes catch us,
    Silencing the murmuring in the theatre.
    We are carried far from concerns of real life,
      Magicked by music.

    As we watch the trivial daily problems –
    Where to place a bed, and a small hat's trimmings –
    Leave the realms of ordinary conversation
      Soaring, transcendent.

    We are made to weep as the Countess wonders
    How she can rekindle her husband's interest.
    We are party to a depraved Count's passions
      Craving indulgence.

    Living out the trials of a young man's fancy,
    Eagerness of bride and impatient bridegroom,
    Torment of a jealous imagination,
      We suffer with them.

    For this night we know of another country,
    Living, breathing fantasy sung and acted.
    We become the confidantes of a people
      Conjured before us.

A single sapphic quatrain does not have a strongly poetic 'feel' about it, but as soon as you produce a poem from a number of these stanzas, the ear becomes attuned to their metre and the poem presents a harmonious whole.

It may feel strange to construct a poem out of a metre where the first syllable of each foot is stressed, because the natural flow of English poetry stresses the second syllable of the foot. It is worth persevering with this form, though, however alien it seems. The resulting poem will be resonant with its own music.

Workshop

Concentrate on the value of cutting. Although it may hurt to remove a single word from your writing, it is important to rid your work of everything that is not essential to convey the mood and message of your subject.

It is not a good idea to begin hacking at your poetry the moment you have placed the last full stop. It is difficult, at this stage, to evaluate the effectiveness of your writing and to know whether the poem can afford to lose anything. Instead go back to poems you have produced in the past.

Start with the gross cuts. Ask yourself whether the poem begins at a telling point, or does it waffle around the subject for a few lines before it starts to make its impact? Any padding can be removed, allowing the impact line its rightful place, at the beginning of the poem. If the extraneous material happens to contain an idea or even just a phrase essential to the comprehension of the poem, remember that that area of the text can be reinstated at a later point.

Look next at the end. Have you stopped when your message was complete? Or is there additional information or explanation after the real close of the poem? You do not need to explain. If your poem is effective, the explanation is unnecessary. Trust your reader's intelligence to supply all he needs for full understanding.

Backtrack for a moment to check the bulk of your poem, all the material within it. Is it entirely relevant to the point you are making and the atmosphere you are creating? Have you wandered off at a tangent or stayed with your subject?

Have you used too many examples, or gone into boring detail? Cut anything you do not need.

After making these gross cuts, work on the fine slices, the slivers. Examine each line of your poem, and every word in the line. Mark all the superfluous matter, then read your poem aloud omitting the marked sections in order to listen to the new effect you have created. Does your poem still make sense? Is it firmer and tighter in this format? If so, cut all the parts you have marked. If not, experiment by reinstating a few of the marked passages. You will soon find the balance point where your poem is telling and also beautifully lean.

If you are unsure about the effects of your cuts, why not practise on somebody else's writing? Take liberties with any published poem you can find, asking yourself how it could be cut, and whether it still works. Your selected poet will never, of course, be aware of the way you are treating his work; but you will gain strong insights into the different effects available to you by attempting such an exercise.

One of the biggest dangers in cutting your writing is that you can hack too fiercely. At every stage in the cutting process you should look back at the original and ask yourself whether you are pruning for the overall health of your poem, or whether you have excised essential material, muddling your message or killing the mood.

Be sure to keep every version of the poem; do not throw one away as soon as you have worked on the next. Then you will be able to make your cuts secure in the knowledge that you can replace, in original or revised form, any material which needs to be returned to your poetry.

Exercises

1   Write a poem on the subject of any sport or leisure activity, and its effect on participants and/or spectators.
2   Devise a list poem. List anything you choose – the con-

tents of a picnic hamper, items which are green in colour, a series of memories from schooldays. You may leave the poem in list form to speak for itself, or add some form of comment which will explain the associations in the catalogue for the reader's benefit.

3   Write a time-slip poem in any form. The idea of this is to create a movement through time, which may be logical or unaccountable. The change in time should be an integral part of the poem.

DAY FOUR

Reading

For this reading exercise, obtain a copy of a collection of poems which were the winners and shortlisted pieces in a competition. These collections are seldom available in bookshops or libraries. They usually need to be ordered directly from the competition's organiser. Check the details on various entry forms to see whether a book is to be produced, and place an order for it. Alternatively, study those magazines which are connected with competitions (e.g. *Envoi*) where winning poems are printed.

To make a proper study of these pieces, you need to cast yourself in the role of adjudicator. Do not merely ask yourself why a poem is good – ask what makes it so much better than all the other entries.

There are likely to be at least three prizewinning poems. Compare and contrast them. Would you have placed them in the same order? If not, why not? Which do you think is going to be the most memorable? Check your choice in a week's time, by recalling as much as you can of all the poems. You may be surprised to discover which one remains most firmly fixed in your mind.

Now look at each of the poems individually, beginning with the first prizewinner. Start with the artistic considerations. What is the poem's theme? Through which areas of subject matter is it conveyed? Does it show originality of initial idea, or an unusual approach to a familiar subject?

Although you cannot know them, make a few guesses

about the thought processes which accompanied the poem's conception. Does it look like an inspired idea, which poured from the writer's pen with hardly a second thought? Is it contrived, possibly gimmicky? Has it an academic 'feel', suggesting that its composer spent a great deal of time and trouble weighing up the contents and theme before setting pen to paper? What impression does it convey to you?

Unless you have an opportunity to talk with the poet, you will never know how close your surmises come to the truth. This is not important. You have made yourself think about the initiation process of the poem, and that is sufficient.

Read it aloud. Is the sound of it aesthetically pleasing? Does it flow? Are its sound effects in harmony with its subject matter?

Look at its appearance on the page. Has the writer started new lines or made stanza breaks at the points you would have chosen? Are the lines of similar length, or widely varied? Does this work with or against the content?

Study the words. Are rhyme, rhythm and metre used effectively? Is the vocabulary exciting? Are literary devices applied with subtlety? Are there any clumsy areas, such as inversions, which might have been ironed out by more thorough revision?

It is likely that your analysis of the poem will lead you to conclude that it has been well thought out and powerfully realised. This is, after all, not just one of a list of selections made by an editor. It is the best of what might have been a very large bunch, picked by an adjudicator seeking something more than excellence. Although his subjective opinion must have been involved in his choice, the quality of the poem should be unmistakable.

Repeat this study with the other prizewinning poems. After you have done so, check again to decide the order in which you would have placed them. Have your ideas changed in the process of analysing them? If so, why?

At the end of your period of heavy study, relax for a while and re-read all the poems purely for the pleasure of reading them. When you move on to the next exercise, you will already be surrounded by the aura of winning poetry.

Writing

Setting out to write a competition poem is a little like setting out to paint a masterpiece or to compose a hit record. You may stumble on a winning formula, but you cannot be sure of the power of your creation. You can, however, load the dice in your favour.

If inspiration should strike, follow the instinct to write exactly what your pen spells out, without conscious effort from your brain. In these fortunate circumstances, do not wait for a convenient writing time. Stop whatever you are doing and write it down.

For the purposes of the exercise, we must assume that inspiration has not struck. If it had, you would be writing by now, not reading this.

Start by working on your idea. No matter how strong your writing, you must have something to say before you begin. Ignore the call of spring and the delights of your garden. Turn your back on your beautiful kitten, red setter or duck-billed platypus. Forget your analysis of man's place in the universe. These are the writing stimuli in everybody's mind. Seek out the unique.

Give your imagination free rein. Do not be satisfied with the things you see and the things you know. Ask yourself the writer's most useful question – 'What if . . .?' – and supply the most bizarre answers you can. Leave those answers for a short while, ask the question again, then look for really bizarre replies. By the time you have reached the realms of the sublime or the ridiculous, you may be coming up with original ideas.

Think of the adjudicator who will be examining your poem. Have your subject matter and intended treatment of it enough to stir his interest? Imagine him working his way through hundreds, or even thousands of stunning entries.

While you are working on the poem, look at every word and phrase you write. Do not let a syllable pass your scrutiny unless it earns its place in your poem. If the competition is fierce, an adjudicator will be delighted to find even the tiniest flaw in a piece of work. It allows him to reject it with a clear conscience in favour of the other excellent poems on offer.

Guard against building obscurities into your work for no other reason than to make you look clever. Check your grammar and punctuation as strictly as you check your vocabulary. Make sure that your writing is never rhyme-led, twisting sense or syntax for the sake of the rhyme. Check that rhythm and metre work, and look at the quantity of material you are putting into your poem. Does it say everything it has to and then end, or do you keep adding extra, unnecessary comment? Does it stop short of communicating your idea?

When you feel you have finished your competition poem, put it away and leave it alone. Take it out at the beginning of your next writing day, and put it through a rigorous revision procedure. Make it fight for its place as your submission to a competition, just as it will have to fight for a prize with every other piece entered.

By the time you have reached the end of the first draft of this poem, you should feel exhausted. Allow yourself a break – this is supposed to be a pleasurable activity, not an exercise in masochism!

Administration

Spend some time sending work off to a range of publishing outlets. It is probably best to begin with the small press magazines ('small' implying the size of the publishing operation, not any slightness in the quality of work used). These magazines are the lifeblood of contemporary poetry, and publish a wealth of big names in the poetry world alongside the work of comparative unknowns. You do not have to be famous, well published, or even a subscriber to the magazine (in most cases) to have your work considered. Acceptance by a range of publications on a regular basis is a tremendous encouragement and will get your work seen by other people in the field.

Prepare your copies as suggested in Day Two, using a new sheet of A4 paper for each, typing it single-spaced, and adding your name and address. (It is important to put this on every sheet. Your copies may become separated from each other in an editorial office.)

Your study of small press magazines will have given you some idea of the best places to send particular areas of material or styles of writing. Group your poems together into batches of no more than six, and select the most suitable outlet for each of the batches.

Send them with a brief and businesslike covering letter, accompanied by a stamped, self-addressed envelope (s.a.e.) of a suitable size for their return, to the appropriate magazine. Be sure to keep a note of their destination. It is amazing how difficult it is to remember which poems went where. The only way to be sure is to keep careful records.

This is where the task of the day ends for the time being. You can spend the rest of your administration time checking through returned poetry, making fresh copies where required, and finding new outlets for work which remains unpublished.

The current exercise continues with the reminder to be patient. You are likely to receive some responses within a few weeks. Others could take months. Make a note of which poems have been accepted, to avoid the embarrassment of sending them elsewhere by mistake, and which have been rejected, to save you from accidentally resubmitting.

Those poems which have been rejected but in which you still have faith should be regrouped into batches for sending to different but still, of course, appropriate outlets – and the process begins again.

Remember that juggling the poems in the batches and trying your work on an ever-increasing number of magazines should not become a substitute for writing fresh material. In fact there is little that is creative about the juggling exercise, but it is essential if you are going to enhance your profile in the world of poetry.

However successful you are with your poetry, small-press magazines offer you a perennial yardstick. Judge by the regularity of your acceptances whether you are maintaining a standard of work, improving on it or falling back.

The selection of your poetry by an independent editor gives you the confidence you need in the work to prompt you to hold it for publication in your next collection.

Fun

One of the most relaxing ways of playing with poetry is to write a parody. Take any thoroughly well-known poem and write a new humorous or satirical version of it in your own words, but using the unmistakable pattern of the original.

Think of the poetry of Lewis Carroll in *Alice in Wonderland*. In one example of a parody he used Jane Taylor's poem, *The Star*, which would be familiar to all his readers:

> Twinkle, twinkle, little star,
> How I wonder what you are!
> Up above the world so high,
> Like a diamond in the sky!

Carroll's version reads:

> Twinkle, twinkle, little bat!
> How I wonder what you're at!
> Up above the world you fly,
> Like a teatray in the sky!

He has repeated the pattern and style of the original, and some of the same vocabulary; but his nonsense version only has appeal for people who know the original, hence the importance of choosing an easily recognised piece. Make a parody of an obscure work by an unknown poet, and its effect falls flat.

The lyrics of W. S. Gilbert, with their irresistible rhythms, make excellent parodies. Play fast and loose with Keats' *Odes*, hefty chunks from Shelley or the richly worded poetry of Dylan Thomas.

Do not feel you have to restrict yourself to poetry of the past. This is just an exercise, not a poem intended for publication. Allow yourself to play with the writing of poets of today, safe in the knowledge that nobody need see the liberties you have taken.

Use the humour of parodies to make a political point or to get your message across forcefully. Familiarity with the style of your medium assists in the business of communication.

Your parody may only be written for your own private enjoyment, or for entertaining a few hand-picked friends with a spoken performance; but it does have a useful purpose to serve. It represents yet another way of exploring the language. By following – as closely as possible – in the footsteps of another poet, you are assimilating aspects of a different style. The fun exercise becomes a challenge from which you will absorb a great deal of knowledge of the working of language.

In addition to the words themselves, you gain experience by mastering the rhythms, metre and rhyme patterns used in your selected poems. You absorb this experience in its most easily digestible form. Because of your total familiarity with the original, you do not have to start counting syllables or checking rhyme schemes. The tune of the poem is already fixed in your head. You just have to make sure that your version of it fits the tune.

Form

Rhyme Royal is a stanza form of seven lines, using three rhymes. It is an ancient pattern, dating back to Chaucer, and usually appears in iambic pentameter. The first and third lines rhyme, the second, fourth and fifth, and the stanza closes with a rhyming couplet. This produces a pattern of:

a b a b b c c

Any number of stanzas in this pattern may be used to create your poem. Their length permits you sufficient space to allow your meaning to unfold, but is short enough to divide your poem into digestible portions.

Example: stanzas from *Plague Village*

The tailor sent to London for a bolt	a
of finest cloth for dressing gentlemen,	b
not dreaming that the worsted for a coat	a
would be the stuff that spread contagion when	b
he measured length for cutting it. But then	b
he did not know his cloth was full of fleas	c
that carried traces of a dire disease.	c
Plague showed itself in fever, coughs and sores.	d
The tailor and his landlady were first	e
to suffer, and as one by one, then scores	d
of friends and neighbours yielded, they grew worse.	e
No family was spared. The village, cursed,	e
saw daily sacrifice; fears multiplied	f
as fathers, mothers, children sickened, died.	f
As fear of the contagion's spreading grew	g
the villagers who chose to meet for prayer	h
decided to avoid the Church, and knew	g
God listened when they met in open air.	h
They walked in silence to the dell, and there	h
sang hymns and psalms, and cried their grief aloud	i
until night's blanket dropped its greying shroud.	i

46

This form is a good vehicle for narrative poetry, but versatile enough to convey most ideas. Experiment by writing humorous poems in this form, or poems expressing two points of view, where a dialogue is set up by assigning alternate stanzas to two characters.

Workshop

Have a look at any poem you produced at least a week ago with a view to revising it into an acceptable form. Revision involves going through every aspect of the poem in order to make as many refinements as possible, but it does not need to be as tedious as it sounds.

Start by reading the poem slowly to yourself. Ask what it is saying to you. Can you remember what you intended it to say at the time when you were writing? Is it conveying the same message, or something else altogether?

It may be that the poem is communicating its intended message with clarity. If so, this is fine. It does not mean that you can skip the rest of the revision process, but you can tackle it with an assurance that the overall effect is the one for which you were aiming.

Do not be alarmed if you have forgotten the original intention, or if your poem does not seem to be conveying its message. Clear your mind of the ideas which surrounded its conception, and ask yourself whether it has anything interesting to say. Does it make its point in an arresting or intriguing fashion? If so, there is no problem. You have satisfied the criterion of having something challenging/absorbing/exciting to put across, whether or not it was the point you originally wanted to make.

The real problems begin if you discover that the poem has little to say and does not say it very well. It is not necessarily a candidate for the shredder, but will need a lot of careful revision before you will feel happy to put your name to it.

Next, try saying the poem aloud. It is surprising how differently it sounds when spoken than when read silently to yourself. Think not so much about the message in your poem as the medium through which it is imparted. Listen for a harmony of sound, the flow of true poetry.

Listen with a willingness to highlight any line, phrase, word or even syllable which does not harmonise with the rest of your poem. Check out the obvious devices, such as rhyming and rhythmic effects, and then look a little deeper. If any single aspect of the poem fails to please, make a note of it. You may be able to put it right on the spot. If not, you will certainly find the task of revision easier at your next attempt if you have marked the flawed areas now.

When you are feeling completely happy with your work as it stands, put your poem away once more. Allow it a little extra time, more breathing space. Look at it again at the beginning of your next writing period. Make any amendments which are necessary for full communication using the perfect words in their most exquisite pattern.

The revision process should be practised repeatedly until you reach a stage where you honestly believe that your poem is as good as it ever will be. If you cast it aside before you reach this stage, you will always feel uncomfortable about the poem. By assuring yourself that you have brought it as close to perfection as you can, you will have a piece of writing of which you can be justly proud.

Exercises

1   Read the first ten poems published in any poetry magazine. Imagine for a moment that you are a competition adjudicator, and that you are reading the entries submitted by competitors. Place the poems in your order of preference, justifying the placings to yourself.
2   Write a short, rhyming poem which depends on a pun to convey its message.
3   Write a narrative poem telling the story of any local tale or legend.

DAY FIVE

Reading

Look at some poetry written during the nineteenth century. Read a number of different poets, and assess your appreciation of each. Ideally, have another glance at the work of poets already familiar to you, and also seek out some unfamiliar names.

Make notes of your observations about subject matter, style, approach and quantity of material in the poems you have chosen to study.

Does anything surprise you about the subject matter? Could you envisage poetry being written on the same subjects today? If so, would it be conveying the same message, or would a different angle be emphasised?

In the matter of style, most poetry of the nineteenth century will, of course, be written in rhymed and metrical forms. Look at the construction of each of your study pieces. Is it written in separate stanzas or in a solid block? Is the chosen pattern appropriate to the subject matter? Are the line lengths fitting? Does the language flow naturally, or has it been twisted in an unusual way to accommodate the elements of rhyme and rhythm? Is the message of the poem conveyed convincingly? Does it say anything worth saying?

What is the angle of approach in each of your poems? Are they told from the point of view you would have expected, or is there an unusual angle? Could you imagine the same material being conveyed from a different point of view? If the poem were being written today, would the same angle be the best to choose?

Examine the quantity of material put across in each poem, and the resulting length of the poem. Are you looking at an epic extending for pages and pages? If so, does it grip you throughout its length, or is it full of unnecessary padding? Do you find it a cohesive, compelling read as a single piece? If its content had been divided into a sequence of poems on the same subject, would you have found it more easily digestible, or merely disjointed?

Your poem might have been a very short one. Does it make its point in a succinct way? Does it make you think? Do you wish the poet had given you more in his writing, or do you prefer to bring your own imagination to furnish further thoughts?

Draw your focus back from the individual poems in order to take a wide view of this period of writing once more. In addition to your perceptions of the poetry, spend a little time thinking about the people who were producing it.

Think of the social and political scenes they experienced. Think about the status of poets during the nineteenth century, and read a little about the lifestyles of some of the great writers of the age.

Think about the original readers of your selected poetry. Who were they? How were their lives different from yours? How different was their basic education from yours? What was their background in literature?

The answers to these last questions will not improve your own writing directly, but the information is fascinating. They will, however, enhance your appreciation of one of the most exciting aspects of poetry, and one of which we should never lose sight. While civilisations exist, poetry will be written. As poets, we are all part of a special fellowship which extends from before the written word through our generation and on for ever.

Writing

The writing exercise for today is not one which can be completed on the spot, as it has a fairly elaborate preparation stage. The idea is to use events in the news as a springboard which will eventually lead to the construction of your next poem. Produce your initial notes now, and add to your material in the days to come.

It is a common reaction to want to write poems commenting on current events, especially if those events are sad or disastrous. Such subjects do not always make the best source material for poems, but they can have a therapeutic value for their writer. Writing about a difficult subject is a good way of coming to terms with it, and coping with the emotions it arouses. Good taste will guide you through the selection process when you are choosing a story to which your poem will respond.

Scour the newspapers, TV and radio bulletins for quirky, witty stories, or look for nuggets of good news that might inspire your writing.

Whatever the nature of your chosen subject matter, resist the temptation to start writing the poem the moment you have selected it. Instead, start making notes, thinking around the subject, exploring it from different viewpoints, trying out different associated ideas. Let your poem evolve out of a combination of growing familiarity with the news story and an in-depth study of potential approaches.

Remember that any news item which prompts you to write will move other people to do so as well. Your developing thought processes become extra specially important. There has to be something about your poem which will make it more telling and thought-provoking than any others rising out of the same source material.

Having made your notes and looked at your potential poem from all angles, keep your mind open for a few days in order to add any follow-up material which appears in the media, and any additional ideas you may wish to include.

While you are thinking about your subject, allow the emotion of the event to flow over you. (There is bound to be an emotional reaction – without it, the event would not have become a news item.) Imagine yourself in the role of somebody affected by the circumstances. Ask yourself how you would act, what you would say and what you would think.

When you actually come to write the poem, immerse yourself simultaneously in the facts, the emotions and the ideas you have been considering. Decide whether you wish to write directly about the event in the news, or to use the information and emotion more obliquely. Transferring your set of ideas into an entirely new range of subject matter can be exhilarating. It also means that your poem no longer relates to one occasion or to one set of circumstances: it has turned into something universal. The factors which prompted it have become no more significant than those which prompt any other poem.

As you write, allow yourself to experiment with different patterns. Free verse, syllabics and a traditionally crafted approach are all worth trying. If the poem falls naturally into one of these options, the choice has been made for you. If it does not, be prepared to play about with different styles until you find the best.

When so much information and thought have gone into a subject, it is a pity to squander all of that on a single poem. Look back at your notes and the accumulated information. Do you have the material for any other writing on the same theme? Do the emotions you wrote about link you to any other, unfamiliar areas of subject matter? Do any associated ideas prompt you to write your next poem?

Remember, the beauty of using news items as source material for your poems is that you are presented with a new supply of subject matter every day. A new set of feelings and reactions will surround every piece you read. Keep your poet's eye open for every piece of writing potential which is delivered to your home, whether in written or in spoken form.

Administration

As soon as you start offering poetry to editors, broadcasters, and competition organisers the need for efficient record-keeping becomes more obvious. The suggestion was made in Day Four that you should be sure to keep a check on the destination of each batch of poems and the results; but it also helps to keep a record of every individual piece.

This record, title-by-title, should be kept in addition to the sorting of finished copies into category files, as described in Day Three.

One of the easiest ways to do this is by using an exercise book with an alphabetical index, like an address book. If you keep your poems in alphabetical order of titles, you can add to each the date when the poem was entered into the files, and dates of any subsequent revisions. It is useful to note the outlets where you have attempted to place a poem, and the results, providing a cross-reference with your destination records (cf. Day Four administration).

If the poem has been sent out to a competition, you can note the closing and judging dates and the name of the adjudicator who has seen it.

If you have an opportunity to read at a class, workshop or writers' circle, you can add brief notes taken from the suggestions offered to you by your tutor or by other writers.

Make a note, too, of audience reaction to your poem. If it produced a ripple of amusement, or even just the 'hmmm' response which indicates that it has made the audience think, you will know that it works well at a reading. Notes reminding you of such responses will help when you are selecting work to read in public on any subsequent occasion.

Another dimension you can record is your own reaction to your poem. If you honestly feel it is good, make an appropriate mark in the book. The next time you are looking for a special poem, perhaps for a competition or submission to an anthology, your eye will automatically light on that piece.

As soon as this poem-by-poem information system is up and running, use it as browsing material. Check the proportion of your poems which have gained some sort of positive response. Try to work out whether these poems have anything in common, e.g. all written during a holiday, all on a particular subject, etc. Your assessment may lead you into a greater awareness of your optimum time to write, most successful subject matter, and other helpful information.

The use of this book does not dispense with the need for cross-referencing. Ideally, you will also have records organised by outlet, so that you can see at a glance which poems have been sent where, and with what results. You may also find it useful to keep chronological records, so that you can check on the expected delay associated with each market, and the time which has elapsed since submitting work to competitions.

The more easily you manage to work the way around your poem titles, the less time you will waste on checking and cross-checking – and, as a direct result, the more time you will have for actually writing your poetry.

Fun

Allow yourself a little light relief by putting a joke into poetry. Recall any joke you have heard which made you laugh aloud. By using the same idea, you are giving yourselt material which is already funny. The trick is to make it even funnier by offering it in the form of a poem.

Jokes are already very close to poetry, mainly because they often depend on a short account, complete in itself and with never a word wasted, in order to create an effect. A brief witticism is comparatively easy to translate into verse form, and can make its point with punch.

For example, consider this joke beloved of the average six-year-old:

'Why do elephants paint the soles of their feet yellow?'
'So they can hide upside down in a bowl of custard.'

You can say exactly the same thing in light verse:

'Can you tell me why elephants constantly paint
The soles of their feet bright as mustard?'

'The answer is simple – it's so they can hide
Upside down in a bowl full of custard.'

The same idea can be put into the limerick form – synonymous with humour – with just a little adaptation:

An elephant, busy and flustered,
Was painting his feet bright as mustard.
   When I said, 'Please explain,'
   He replied, 'Use your brain –
It's to hide in a bowl full of custard.'

As soon as you use any verse form to convey your joke, you
are making it more memorable and giving an extra dimension
to the humour. If you have the ability to think up your own
jokes rather than rely on old chestnuts such as this example,
so much the better.

It is easier to write in some form of poetry which uses
rhyme and metre than in free verse when you want to tell a
joke with panache. This is possibly because the tripping effect
of the rhythm contributes to the overall effect of the joke.
Experiment with different verse patterns to find the one
which best fits your subject matter and style of telling.

Do remember that the effectiveness of a regular beat and
full rhyming pattern will be weakened as soon as you allow
either to slip. The joke is not an occasion for artistic
variations in metre and rhyme. It will be all the funnier if it
is slick and conforms precisely to the pattern the listener's ear
expects.

Form

The tanka is a Japanese syllabic form of poetry. It usually
consists of a single stanza of five lines, the lines consisting of
five, seven, five, seven, and seven syllables respectively. It is
unrhymed, and the form does not impose any metrical
restrictions.

The tanka may be written as two distinct blocks separated by white space. In this case, there is a turn – a slight shift in sense or emphasis – after the first three lines, which end with a noun or verb, before the final two lines.

Example:

> Bud of daffodil
> bursts from its parchment wrapping,
> a cracked Easter egg.
>
> Trumpets herald gold summer,
> bray their arc to link fruit fall.

A tanka produced by two poets is known as a renga, the first poet writing the opening three lines, the second adding the couplet.

Syllabic poetry offers the writer a distinct opportunity to examine the words he is using in order to make the best possible use of the few syllables at his disposal. This discipline is invaluable for poets. Poetry which involves a syllable count, whatever other restrictions it may offer in terms of form, is an admirable exercise to practice.

Workshop

Selection of vocabulary is a vital task for a poet. Dealing in a craft where precision is essential, he must be certain that every word he picks is the best possible choice to convey his meaning. At the same time, he is looking for language which transcends the banal, and yet does not smack of affectation.

Words should be absolutely correct, and verified with the dictionary if necessary; but they should also reflect the living use of language. They should be chosen with instinct and flair.

On those extremely rare occasions when a poem is bursting to be written and you canot hold yourself back from spilling it on to the page, it would be crazy to stem the flow in order to rifle the thesaurus. Let the words pour, knowing that there will be plenty of revision time available to change any that do not fit when the flood of creativity has abated.

You may be surprised, on such occasions, to discover how few words need changing. It is as if your mind, muse, inspiration or whatever you name it, is presenting you with the poem in a near-perfect form. This does not mean you should by-pass the revision process. Check out every word, make changes where necessary, and be thankful for anything you have written which works without alteration.

If the production of the poem is a more arduous task, it is likely that the vocabulary of your first draft will need a fair amount of attention. You may even find it useful to ring, as you write, every word which does not seem to be the perfect choice for its place. With problem words already highlighted, you have an easy route to check through the poem.

In addition to concentrating on the key words of your poem and their effectiveness, be on guard against the seven deadly sins of vocabulary for the poet. These are:

1 Highly poetic language. A vocabulary spattered with miasmas, seraphim and myriad is suspect.
2 Archaisms. Avoid 'tis, 'twas, thou and whene'er at all costs.
3 Abstract terms. 'Beautiful' and 'majestic' are fine for guide books, but offer the poet none of the required precision in expressing thoughts.
4 Adjectives. There is nothing wrong with the adjective as such, but poets may fall prey to the temptation to stuff great wads of them into their more descriptive lines. One apposite example is sufficient in most cases.
5 Adverbs. These need to be treated with greater caution. It is usually better to seek out a more precise verb than to qualify a general one with an adverb.
6 Clichés. Beware the words which have been used a

thousand times to convey your message. Search a little more deeply to come up with a surprising alternative.

7 Repetitions. Some repetition works perfectly as a poetic device, but there are occasions when a repeated word suggests that its writer could not come up with anything new. There is too much emphasis on every single word in a poem for an unwarranted repetition to slip by unnoticed. Watch, too, for repetition of little working words, such as the definite article. Its overuse can become tedious.

The attraction of all these rules is the fact that poetry thrives without legislation. In other words, these guidelines are for general application. Every poem is a unique entity. Its strength may depend on your flouting one or all of the 'rules' on a particular occasion.

Use the time when you are not writing poetry to consider your vocabulary. As a poet, you are already likely to be fascinated by anagrams and word games. Spend time playing with the sounds of words, exploring the pleasure of onomatopoeia, where sense is buttressed by the sound a word makes in pronunciation. Invent new words, and devise new uses for familiar ones. Explore the vocabulary of a chosen subject, noting any words which have a double meaning. Make word lists and doodle pictures out of words.

These exercises are not designed to force you into using an artificial and convoluted vocabulary. They are simply making you more aware of the beauty and versatility of the language in which you are writing. Enjoy handling the tools of your poetic trade.

Exercises

1   Take any poem written in the nineteenth century. Update it, keeping the message the same but using today's vocabulary and terms of reference.

2   Make a list of grammatical errors, words and phrases which grate on you in ordinary conversation. Now list those which you find difficult to tolerate in poetry. (This is not a memory test – look through as many books as you wish.) Finally check your own poetry, both to make sure that you have not used any of the expressions in your own lists, and to discover whether you are making heavy use of expressions which might irritate other people.

3   Write a rhymed poem suitable for inclusion in a greetings card. Its messsage may be sincere or jokey. Would you send that particular message to anybody? If so, to whom? If you have the courage of your convictions, buy a blank card and pen your own words.

DAY SIX

Reading

Many poems have been written in response to other works of
art. There are poems commenting on paintings, statues, plays
and pieces of music. Browse through a few books, and you
are likely to find a good selection of poetry based on the arts.

Read each poem carefully. Are you familiar with the work
which initiated it? If you are, do you see a striking similarity
between the poem and the original work? Or was the original
no more than a spur forcing the poet away at a tangent? Can
you follow the thought processes which guided the poet? Or
do you see no logical links between the original work and the
poem?

Look a little closer. Does the original piece inspire the
same feelings and emotions in you as the poem? Are there
structural similarities between the two works (e.g. a poem
written in response to a piece of music, where fast and
slow passages and separate movements are indicated in
both)?

Try to imagine yourself as the poet. Would his ideas about
the original work have entered your head? Could you imagine writing a poem similar to his, or would yours have followed entirely different lines?

Finally, ask yourself which you prefer – the original work
or the poem? This is a difficult question. It is like being asked

61

to choose between cheese and chocolate: the choice depends on your mood, the time of day and all sorts of other factors. By stating a preference to yourself, however subjective, you are merely ordering your thoughts at that precise moment.

It could be that you have never encountered the original work which inspired the poem. If this is the case, ask yourself whether the poem works without knowledge of its source. If the answer to this is yes, the poem may be said to be successful. The poet drew on an area of source material, and then, during its creation, the poem outgrew its reliance on the source material. If your answer is no, then a dimension of enjoyment of the poem has been lost. This does not mean the poem has failed, but that its creator perhaps relied just a little too heavily on the presence of the original work, rather than transferring its dynamics into the poetry.

Think, too, of the process in reverse. Do you know of any statues or paintings that were produced directly in response to a piece of poetry? Is their appeal enhanced or diminished by being part of a set of work?

It is an added bonus to study pieces where the poet and the originator of the work of art are one. Look at the work of Dante Gabriel Rossetti for an example of an artist/poet who believed that his ideas were incomplete until he had explored them through both spheres of creativity.

If you are fortunate enough to be creative in more than one area, study pieces you yourself have produced in the past. Are there any intended links between poems and pieces of music you have written, collages you have made, sketches you have drawn? Can you discern links that were unintentional? Do associated creations rely on each other to be appreciated to the fullest extent, or does each stand significantly alone?

There are no right or wrong answers to any of these questions. They are simply designed to concentrate the focus of your attention, and to work out which approaches hold the greatest appeal for you.

Writing

It is a fascinating exercise to write a poem based on a picture. Choose your picture first, and select it with care. It may be a postcard-sized representation of an old master, a contemporary painting, a snapshot, even a drawing done by a small child. A picture which you like or which makes you think is the best subject.

Start by making general notes about your picture. Detail its subject matter, colours, and the mood it invokes in the observer. Is there a story inherent in it? Does it please or disturb? Why did you choose it?

As soon as you have completed this basic analysis, start writing your poem. Your ideas have probably not been fully developed yet, but that does not matter. There is room for spontaneity and instinct in the most carefully considered writing exercises.

Equally it does not matter, at this stage, precisely what you are writing down. One thing to remember from the beginning is that your writing will start to assume the shape of a poem if you produce it in lined form, rather than in a solid paragraph. Take a new line for each turn of thought.

Write as quickly as you can, letting instinct take over whenever your conscious thoughts begin to flag. Try to resist the temptation to read over what you have written. Concentrate on a constant motion forward.

Keep looking at your picture, and be aware all the time of the effect it is having upon you. As you write, do you feel more or less comfortable with the picture? Does it still look the same, or have any aspects of it apparently changed? Is your emotional reaction the same as when you began, or has it altered as your thoughts about the picture have been allowed to flow?

When your writing loses tempo, read slowly over the lines you have produced. Are they in full accord with your appreciation of the picture? Have you written anything which surprises you? Have you explored areas of writing which you have covered before, or are you moving into new spheres?

By this time you should have your brief initial notes and an expanded mass of lines prompted by your picture, even though they may have moved a considerable distance from the original source material. It is time to start shaping them into a poem.

It is likely that the form your poem will take has been developing – with or without your knowledge – while you wrote. Do you have a series of long lines with the general feel of a particular metre? Are your lines irregular? Is there any element of rhyme, either full or slant?

Does the shape of your lines harmonise in any way with the pattern of your picture? For example, if the picture is of a sweeping landscape, are your lines long and flowing? If the picture is a stark abstract, are they short and staccato? By checking for such unconsciously produced features in your extended notes, you are following your instinct in the matter of form.

Keep your source picture in your line of sight while you work on the poem. Select areas from your notes which best relate your reactions to the picture, creating a harmonious entity out of your rough ideas. At the end of the first draft, discard the picture. From now on, your poem will stand or fall without this prop.

When you have worked on the writing in your usual way and refined it into a poem which satisfies you, look again at your picture. Do the two works of art complement each other? Are their links obvious, suggested, or non-existent?

Finally, ask yourself whether your poem stands on its own. Does it have anything to communicate? Does it speak out effectively? Remember that it does not need to carry a weighty message. A poem may be no more than the cameo of a moment, describing a brief scene, a passing thought, the momentary view of a character. At the opposite extreme, it may hold an internationally vital message, or transmit the most profound feelings a human being could possibly experience. Communication exists when something – anything – is conveyed from the poet via his words to the reader.

Administration

As somebody who enjoys writing poetry, you are probably
keen to look out for general information connected with the
subject, such as TV and radio programmes about poets. It is
a worthwhile activity to keep an anthology file of all the snip-
pets of information you can find.

Use the file to collect appropriate features from writers'
magazines and small-press poetry publications. Take notes
whenever you come across a programme connected with poetry. It may mar your enjoyment of a broadcast in the short
term, but will be sure to prompt your memory in the future,
bringing the programme to life every time you glance at the
notes.

Similarly, take notes at any talks, readings, workshops or
seminars you attend. Reflecting on these can have a revitalis-
ing effect on your work.

Keep in the anthology file any poems you come across and
enjoy outside the 'permanent' setting of a book, i.e. published
in newspapers or magazines. It is too easy to lose unattached
copies or accidentally throw magazines away.

Make copies of stories which feature poetry in some way,
or write notes about them for your file.

Keep cuttings of material you discover in general publications which relates to poets or any aspect of poetry. It may
be a report about teaching the subject in schools, a review of
a major new collection, even a cartoon strip mentioning a
poem.

Add greetings cards whose verses bring you pleasure, texts
or mottoes which make you think, scraps of paper bearing
'found' poems, their wording being an unconscious creation
of poetry.

Collect poetry 'one-liners' – those tiny nuggets of information which are irrelevant but intriguing. In short, hold within
your anthology file as much and as varied material as you
can find.

One of the joys of this sort of file is a haphazard approach
to the collection it contains. If you have an orderly mind, you

might find it frustrating to jumble your material together willy-nilly. If tidiness does not concern you too much, throw everything in together. You will have an added bonus in the serendipity of drawing items out at random and considering them in context with each other.

The object of collecting items is simply to provide yourself with a fund of material related to poetry. Dip into it at any time for its amusement and fascination value.

As you dip, keep your mind open to the possibility that your next poem could be taking shape deep within you, prompted by this steeping yourself in the whole business of poetry. If that should happen, the result more than justifies the small amount of effort required to set up the file. If it should not, you have enjoyed a few minutes spent in the company of poetry – and there is no better company than that.

Fun

Although spatial poems are not universally popular with editors, they are pleasurably challenging to devise and can be exhibited to striking effect.

Example: *Diamond*

she
wanted his
time honeyed days
nights of silk sheets champagne
and jewels cascading through her fingers
she wanted a diamond solitaire to hold him to those
promises he made not a mound of excuses
nor weekends with his foul kids
showing her she
didn't want
him

A spatial poem depends on its physical appearance on the page to make an impact. The appearance makes its mark on the reader even before the poem is read, creating an image in the reader's mind. It can take one of two forms.

The calligramme is printed in the form of a block of text. The shape of either the block of printed text or of the spaces it creates reinforces the message of the words, as above.

The words of a concrete poem form a complementary picture.

Example: *Worm*

early
    bird
        pecks prompt
            seeking
e a r t h   s a f e   g r o u n d   s a f e   e a r t h   s a f e
           w   ms   gg ng ee   lo
          or   wi   li   fr   be   w

Having produced your spatial poem, you should endeavour, as part of the creative act, to present it in an intriguing way. If you are artistic, you might make a picture or a poster of your poem which could be put on display.

Merely exhibiting your poem in ordinary printed form is rewarding. A simple, typed sheet can be mounted on card and framed.

This may sound like a lot of trouble to bring one poem to public attention, but it is a fact that the markets for spatial poetry are limited. If you can make a talking point of your poem by hanging it on a wall in your own home, you have succeeded in making it communicate.

The treatment of your poem does not have to be large scale. Poems which are brief enough can be produced on a bookmark or even a keyring, or used to decorate a notebook.

This unusual presentation of your poetry is not suggested

as a mere gimmick. A small gift incorporating one of your poems in this way could be more appreciated for the thought and care that went into its production than for its intrinsic value.

Spatial poems written for children make a special present, or could be used in a birthday card to be cherished for years to come.

Conceive your poems and their intended method of presentation as a single entity, and you will have discovered a new dimension to the pleasures of writing poetry.

Form

The English ode is a thirty-line poem written in iambic pentameter. In this form, a poet dispenses with the complexities of construction inherent in odes modelled on the Greek dramatic style.

There are three stanzas in the English ode, the rhyme pattern for each being:

a b a b c d e c d e

Example: *On Botticelli's St Sebastian*

One image lasts when hundred others fade.	a
The young man, tree-bound, hands behind his back	b
in attitude more careless then dismayed,	a
is pierced about with arrows. Here the rack	b
of pain is scorned. He shows no sign of fear.	c
His haloed head is tilted, dead eyes scan	d
unseeing. His defiance is control;	e
his martyrdom is not quiescence. Here	c
is soldier braving death, and here is man,	d
near naked, vulnerable flesh and soul.	e

Behind him horsemen bear their arms away,	f
a lover languishes upon the grass,	g
the cliff path winds to join the sweep of bay	f
and towers and trees reach up through sky's	
gold glass.	g
On backdrop bands of alternating shade	h
of amber, green, blue, grey, Sebastian grafts	i
unconquered domination, prompting all	j
that is not part of suffering to fade	h
in shadows while his torment glows, and shafts	i
of arrows wail the waste their tips despoil.	j

This picture will not slip away from me	k
as others from my mind. It will recur	l
to prick with points of shared pain; memory	k
will sharpen focus when its details blur.	l
He holds me slave through power I can't deny;	m
his form consumes my mind, his gaze implores	n
confession of the faith that saw him slain.	o
Five hundred years divide us, but the tie	m
his artist forged is fresh and binding, draws	n
response each time I try to lose his pain.	o

The English ode is a weighty pattern of poetry which therefore lends itself to fairly serious subject matter. It is a useful vehicle for material which you feel would fit into sonnet form, but which requires a lengthier treatment.

Workshop

Look carefully through the poems you have written at some time in the past to consider the message you are conveying in them, and their overall sense of balance.

These poems will probably have been subjected to revision at least once before, but the revision process concentrates, quite rightly, on the fine details of the construction of poetry.

It is necessary to step back from time to time, and examine the work you are creating in general terms.

Initial revision will have highlighted the area of message you wished to communicate. Now look at your poem as a whole and ask yourself precisely what it is saying to you. Do not concentrate only on the theme, but also on the subject matter which gives texture to your theme. Are subject and theme compatible? What type of effect does the message impose on you? It may prompt a strong emotional reaction or merely draw your attention to something trivial.

Without agonising over any individual words and phrases, ask yourself whether you have included the correct quantity of material in your poem. Is enough said to ensure that the reader knows what you are trying to put across? Have you avoided the temptation to say too much? Remember the value of leaving a little to the reader's imagination. If everything is stated in detail, there is no room for question marks, enigmas or personal responses to imagery.

Look at the way you have balanced your poem. Has the subject matter been injected in a steady stream throughout? Are there areas crammed with detail? Then others where the reader's mind is allowed to wander because the poem does not seem to have anything concrete to say?

Assess your own reactions after reading the poem. Do you feel almost breathless with the effort to keep up with its pace? Are you metaphorically dragging your heels, longing for something to happen?

These are all extreme cases. If you are at all uncomfortable about quantity and balance of material, remember that any of these examples can apply to a lesser degree.

Having pinpointed a problem area in balance, you will be able to remedy it with just a little effort. Edge into slightly different areas of subject matter, trim or expand on your material until the stuff of your poem will fit more comfortably within its chosen pattern.

There is one word of warning to note. Remember that it is impossible to use self-assessment as a reliable means of judging your work, even in the generalised area considered here.

However much you distance yourself from the writing, the fact that you are analysing your own words gives you a built-in advantage. Then again, you are not in the business of pulling your writing to pieces for no good reason. Acting as your own critic, be honest about your shortcomings, also be rational and gentle on yourself.

Exercises

1 Write a short, rhyming poem about any place you dislike, (continents distant or in your immediate vicinity).
2 Take the title of any poem you have read and make an anagram from it. Write a free verse poem which links the theme of the original title with that of the anagram.
3 Write a poem condensing the story of any novel you have enjoyed into a maximum of twenty lines, using rhyme or free verse.

DAY SEVEN

Reading

Explore some metaphysical poetry. This is the poetry of metaphor, practised by the writers of the early seventeenth century, where compressed meanings were expressed through unconventional images. These included the imagery of the poets' ordinary daily life, and also of the art, culture, science, discoveries and philosophies of their time. Start, maybe, with poems by the founder of that school of writing, John Donne, and then read the work of Andrew Marvell, George Herbert, Henry Vaughan, etc.

The extended images and complex conceits of these poems, combined with a dramatic style of writing, make the whole school as vibrant as it is difficult. It is possible to spend more time trying to work out all the convoluted nuances of meaning than actually enjoying your reading of the poems.

Perhaps the most useful insight these works offer to the practising poet of today is their awareness of the time in which they were written. Metaphysical poetry is crammed with allusions to contemporary scientific discoveries. It is full of references to the trades and crafts of the age. It stands as a monument to the thinking of the early seventeenth century.

Think a little about this awareness of time. The poems being written today are fixed within their own timescale. This is one of the strengths of our craft. There is a wonderful sense of continuity in this specific fixing of poetry. You are aware of poets of the past adding their input to the sum total of poetry created, and that future writers will be making their own contributions. You are creating literary history here and now with the poems you write.

It is important to write in the style and idiom of today. Though it is fine to make use of the forms from the past which have been adapted and refined into perfect vehicles for conveying a poem's message, remember that the use of antiquated language will make your poem seem dated before it is even fully realised.

A poem will have immediacy and a sense of modernity if it uses contemporary references and subject matter in a contemporary voice; but consider this note of warning: there is one aspect of metaphysical poetry which is not so attractive. Metaphysical poems were written by clever and learned poets who appeared to build obscurity into their writing for its own sake. To understand them, a reader had to be able to analyse them intelligently and pick up difficult references; to be well-versed in the most recent scientific discoveries, and have a broad general knowledge. The implication was that the reader had to be on an intellectual par with the writer, and that poetry was the reward for an élite, not the right of every man and woman. This alienating attitude prevailed long after metaphysical poetry ceased to have a strong following.

Writing

Work on some syllabic poetry, where the rhyme and metre, if any, are less important than a particular pattern of syllables in the poem.

There are many set forms of syllable count poetry, the Japanese ones, perhaps, being the most regularly practised, but much Celtic poetry is also written in syllabics. While it is engaging and valuable to be familiar with these forms, devising your own syllabic pattern is especially rewarding. Writing a few words and then setting them out in different combinations of syllabic lines offers intriguing insights into your emerging poem.

The simplest form to explore first is normative syllabics, where the same number of syllables occurs in each line of the poem, and the poem may be of any length. Consider these lines:

> This house stands where sea
> once lapped on the shore,
> foundations weighted
> deep packed sand its rock.
> Chambers ventilate
> where fish explored weed;
> boards float in this earth
> which was crest of wave,
> side-scuttle of crab.

The only element of harmony in their construction is the count of five syllables to a line. If you glance at the first few lines, this structure is unlikely to have an impact as a poem. The more lines you read, however, the stronger the poetic effect.

Look at the same words written in the form of quantitative syllabics, where the first stanza lays down a pattern of syllable numbers to the line. This is then repeated in each subsequent stanza:

> This house stands
> where sea once lapped
> on the shore, foundations weighted
>
> deep packed sand
> its rock. Chambers
> ventilate where fish explored weed;
>
> boards float in
> this earth which was
> crest of wave, side-scuttle of crab.

As you will see, the words fit quite happily into 3–4–8 syllable count tercets, although it would make sense to adjust the wording of the final stanza in order to avoid using the weak word 'in' at the strong line-end point. The appearance of the lines takes on an undeniable 'look' of poetry.

The same words constructed in variable syllabics would loosen the format. The syllable count is not set for each line in this form, but must remain within certain parameters chosen by the poet. In this example, there will be no fewer than three and no more than nine syllables in each line:

> This house stands
> where sea once lapped on the shore,
> foundations weighted deep
> packed sand its rock. Chambers ventilate
> where fish explored weed; boards
> float in this earth which was crest
> of wave, side
> scuttle of crab.

The sense of the words remains the same, but their dynamics have been altered once again.

Syllabic forms lend themselves to the construction of found poems. When you come across a portion of poetic prose which you feel would work as a poem, divide it into lines using one of the three disciplines demonstrated. The effect can be fascinating.

Whether you are using found material or devising your own lines, experimentation in different patterns will show you the most appropriate format for conveying your message.

Administration

In Day Four we considered the production of poetry which

is suitable for competitions. Although this artistic side of the competition business is the vital one, it is important to keep the administrative side of competing up to date.

Poetry competitions proliferate, and can become an important outlet for your work. A poem which is published gives you a buzz of satisfaction and the incentive to write and submit more. A poem which wins a competition prize provides the excitement and accompanying incentive in tenfold measure. It may also provide the element which is spectacularly lacking from most of one's dealings with poetry: money.

Look out for information about poetry competitions in all sources. Many smallpress magazines list forthcoming competitions and may include fliers giving entry details. General writers' magazines offer the same information. Leaflets are sent out to libraries and arts centres, which should be checked regularly.

These are the best sources of information about the standard literary competitions, many of which are held annually. Do not neglect occasional or one-off competitions. Keep an eye on local and national newspapers to learn about them. Watch out for them in general interest magazines, Teletext, radio broadcasts and leaflets in shops. Your chances may be enhanced where advertising reaches the public at large rather than just the specialised – and expert – readership of writing magazines.

Send an s.a.e. for information about every competition that interests you, then collect all your entry details together and store them in chronological order of closing date. There is nothing more frustrating than writing a piece specifically for a competition which closed last month.

At the same time, prepare and be ready to keep up to date a file on those poems which you believe might have a good chance in competitions. Keep them together both to provide you with a large choice of work from which to select entries, and to make sure you do not inadvertently send any of them out for magazine publication. As soon as the poem has been published, it renders itself ineligible for most competitions.

Choose your work with care. Consider the nature of the

competition itself. Look at the organisers, and decide whether it would be appropriate to submit work which would appeal directly to them. For example, if the competition is being held for the benefit of a charity for elderly people, poetry touching on the concerns of the aged may be specially welcome. Look at the adjudicator and study his own style of writing. Then read through your potential submissions to see if any might have strong appeal.

Make your submissions well within the deadline but remember that the earlier you send in your work, the longer it will be tied up before you learn its fate. Remember, too, that by holding back your entry until, say, a month before the closing date, you are giving yourself time to produce a better or more appropriate poem for the occasion.

Check the competition rules in minute detail before entering. Requests for a particular style of presentation, multiple copies, and cheques payable to a certain name are made to ease the practicalities of organisation. Rules requiring unpublished poetry which is not currently on offer elsewhere are to avoid the adjudicator's and the poet's potential embarrassment, and to ensure anonymity. If a certain form or theme is demanded, only poems fitting these conditions are required.

If you ignore any of the rules, you are merely wasting your time and money. You worked hard to create the best possible poem for the competition. Do not spoil its chances by cutting corners at the submission stage.

Be sure to keep records of your competition work and its whereabouts. You need to know when you can consider it free for submitting elsewhere. If the entry form does not give a date when the adjudication will be over, allow at least three months to elapse after the closing date.

If they are to be made available, do make sure that you obtain a copy of the results, winning poems and judge's report. You will be able to assess current trends in the competition world and, more importantly, you will learn about the adjudicator's preferences and prejudices. File this information carefully. Poets who are willing to adjudicate are invited to judge competitions over and over again. The more you learn about them, the better your chances of picking appropriate poems to send them.

Fun

Too many of us are closet poets, keeping our writing activities a well-guarded secret. Drawing attention to poetry will increase public awareness of this very special art form. Be prepared to talk about your poetry wherever you go. Watch the reactions when you unleash a stream of poetry on to unsuspecting friends.

Use this part of your writing day to plan a campaign of publicity to promote the interests of poetry in general and your material in particular. Draw up a list of ideas which will attract attention to your writing, and put aside any vestiges of modesty or reticence. Here are a few thoughts to start your list.

Have a supply of short poems which put their message across powerfully or wittily. Add a copy of one of these to every letter you send out to a friend, keeping a selection of suitable material to slide into greetings cards. For Christmas you can produce a special topical piece to include with your correspondence.

Write poems to accompany photographs you show to people. Try to produce a poem for every picture in your album, remembering that the short and punchy will be read and enjoyed – the long and rambling will be ignored. However well they are written, to the non-poet they will be more boring than 60 assorted snaps of somebody else's children.

Have your shortest poems printed on your personal cards for informal contacts, or as part of the heading on your stationery. Desk-top publishing has made an effective means of diplaying poems simplicity itself.

Be prepared to share news concerning your poetry. Find a friendly contact in the offices of your local newspaper and report any spectacular successes. A single poem in a magazine may not be newsworthy, but publication of a collection, work appearing in a large anthology, a competition win, or a public reading deserves recognition. Ask your contact whether you should speak to a reporter or prepare your own press release. Whichever you do, be sure to have a photograph you can offer for publication alongside the text.

Try to make contact with other poets in your area, bearing in mind that combined efforts are more effective and more fun than a lone voice. Arrange to correspond or to meet. If there is no poetry workshop group in your town, investigate the possibility of starting one for mutual help and support, or to co-operate in the production of publications. If a group already exists, seek it out and join it.

Having compiled your list, and added far more imaginative ideas than the ones suggested here, put your thoughts into practice. These ideas are not simply an exercise in egotism. They are avenues into the advancement of poetry generally within the community, and into the development of your own writing. Support them with pride.

Form

Ottava rima is an Italian form much used by Byron. A single stanza, which is eight lines long, may stand on its own as a complete poem, or any number of stanzas may comprise the poem.

It is written in iambic pentameter. Lines one, three and five rhyme together, as do lines two, four and six. The final two lines form a rhyming couplet. This creates a rhyme pattern of:

a b a b a b c c

Example: stanzas from *Byron in Venice*

First drawn by water, he who on the land   a

was clumsy, whose lame foot set him apart,	b
had found the element he could command.	a
Along the cool canals he'd swim, and dart	b
with speed and grace. By night, a torch in hand	a
aloft to warn the gondoliers, he'd part	b
the lapping waters. In the day he'd float	c
above them, his reflections for a boat.	c
And love came soon for one whose strong desire	d
was never sated. With his change of scene	e
he found a mistress burning with a fire	d
to match his own, a gipsy-featured queen.	e
Her husband, taking horns for his attire,	d
respected custom, did not intervene	e
to break the match. His baser instincts fed,	f
Lord Byron sought more solace out of bed.	f
By day he joined the holy brotherhood	g
for talk and contemplation, and to learn	h
their tongue. On St Lazzaro long he stood	g
within the convent garden, or he'd turn	h
his gaze across the water, watch tide flood	g
and ebb until the sun had dropped to burn	h
the sea. By night the furious revelry	i
unmasked some remnants of nobility.	i

This multiple stanza form is a useful vehicle for narrative poetry. The single stanza allows you to make a point neatly and succinctly, summing it up with the sense of finality imbued by the rhyming couplet in the last two lines.

Workshop

Think about the effectiveness with which you communicate emotion – authentic feeling rather than sentimentality. Poetry is perhaps the easiest form of writing in which to express your own passions. Because poetry digs so deeply into the soul of the writer, it is natural that emotional depth should result. It is also possible to hold back, depriving the reader of full comprehension of your sensitivities.

If you are writing directly about a personal experience, the knowledge of the sensations you felt at the time is stored alongside your memories. It is as important to recall emotion as to recollect the facts you are communicating. Delve into your memory, however painful it may be, to remember the truth of the associated emotions.

Just as the facts of a personal experience may be altered or commented upon for artistic effect in a poem, so your inner response to these episodes may be treated with poetic licence. By reliving the genuine feelings associated with your experience, you will be able to attempt with sincerity those adjustments necessary for the production of a good poem.

If your poem deals not with events but with your observations and philosophy, you should still tap into your emotional resources to be sure that you analyse the passion of your reactions to the subject matter.

The poem may deal with material which is totally outside your sphere. If this is the case, you can use two elements to contribute to the veracity of impassioned input. These are your imagination, working overtime while you explore vicariously the subject matter of your poem, and your own store of emotional memory, investigated to match feelings you have known at first hand with material unfamiliar to you.

Look back through poems you have written to see how strongly your feelings have been conveyed. Analyse your own reactions when you relive the poems as their reader rather than their writer. Have you ever relied on clichés to communicate universally understood feelings? Or have you tried to look more deeply, finding original means of expression? Have you avoided ardent reaction, or skirted around it? Would the poem have been stronger if it had contained more fervour? Would the reader's reaction have been enhanced by a stronger content of emotion?

Strong emotional content is not a prerequisite for a good poem. In fact the strength of some poetry relies on its dispassionate conveying of information. But if you feel that a poem is a touch too remote and fails to arouse a responsive sensation in the reader, it could be that an injection of genuine feeling is needed.

Exercises

1   Present yourself with two words chosen at random by sticking a pin in a dictionary. Allow yourself a minute's brainstorming for each – writing down every word or phrase that comes into your head, whether or not it has any logical connection with the starter word. Look at your two lists, and create a poem which links ideas taken from both.
2   Write a poem inspired by anything that happened to you yesterday. The poem may relate the experience, or appear to be completely unconnected with it.
3   Allow yourself a timed period of 15 minutes in which to write a complete poem about any topic – with the exception of the difficulty of writing a poem in 15 minutes.

DAY EIGHT

Reading

Relax for a while with a large anthology of poetry. Select a
book which covers a wide span of time and includes a good
number of poets.

On this occasion, try to suspend the poet's natural curiosity with regard to the construction and thought processes
that went into creating the poems. Read purely to enjoy.

Dip into different areas of the book to make sure that you
get the flavour of each period of writing, if the collection is
presented in chronological order. Relish the sense of continuity, as one age gives way to the next and the poetry survives.

Do not spend too much time trying to sort out the precise
meaning of any poem which raises questions in your mind.
Rather, make a virtue of these questions. Allow something of
the enigma which is part of the magic of poetry to seep into
you, and take pleasure from any 'incomplete' readings. The
chances are that your questions will resolve themselves the
next time you turn to the poems that prompted them. It is as if
a part of your mind holds your questions and considers them
without any conscious thought on your part. You come back
to the poem, and the problem is solved – just as you can leave
a crossword puzzle you have been working on unsuccessfully,
but when you return to it the answers are clearer in your mind.

While you are browsing, read an occasional poem aloud.
Listen as much to its sound effects as to its message. Feel its
rhythm flowing through you. Enjoy the sensation of its words
in your voice.

Make notes of poems which have an immediate effect on you. If you are stirred to excitement, contentment, anger, etc. by anything you read, jot down its title. It may be worth more detailed study another day.

Note, too, any previously undiscovered writers whose poetry you read. List poems which are new to you by familiar writers you have studied before.

At the end of your reading period, put the book down for a few moments and then try to recall by author and title as many of the poems as you can. Which remains most firmly fixed in your mind?

Of the poems you remember most clearly, ask yourself why they made such a strong impression on you. If you followed the advice at the beginning of this reading period, you will not have analysed any of the work in great detail. You are looking for gut reaction, rather than a reasoned appreciation of a poem's subject or construction.

Take the one poem which is clearest in your mind and return to it. How accurately had you remembered it? Does a second reading alter its impact? Do you think you will return to it again, at some time in the future? If it is a very special piece, make a copy of it for your anthology file.

Writing

Whether or not it is your preferred style, write some rhyming poetry. You may wish to use a traditional set form which incorporates rhyme, or simply to place rhymes where they seem correct throughout your poem. Whichever technique you adopt, see it through so that your rhymed poetry has a harmony of style.

While writing in rhyme, be aware of the metrical balance of your lines. It is a perfectly legitimate procedure to write rhyming poetry with lines of irregular lengths and stress patterns. If, however, you impose a metrical pattern on your poem, be sure to adhere to it.

Start by using some full rhyme, where matching sounds chime against each other, such as game/flame or slay/pray. Remember that your poem should never be rhyme-led. The rhymes will only work if their words are the best possible choice for expressing your message. As soon as you compromise your intended meaning for the sake of sound, you weaken your poem. Do it too frequently, and you make a nonsense of the whole piece.

For example, suppose that you were writing a poem in praise of the springtime – a difficult challenge in itself, as this subject has been used so frequently that finding an original angle is quite a problem. You might start with the line:

Green buds piercing through the earth

and then require a rhyme for it. A logical, natural progression for this subject matter might be:

Remind us of the year's rebirth.

This is not an inspired idea, but it fits the intended theme and could be worked into the poem in a convincing manner. Imagine that this idea did not present itself. We could end up with:

Fill us all with joy and mirth

or

Show how much joy our garden's worth

or

Compensate for winter's dearth

or even

Make our town prettier than Perth.

To anyone with the slightest sense of poetry, the alternatives are laughable. They are weak, meaningless and irrelevant in the context of the poem's intended theme. The only thing in their favour is that the rhyme fits. This is not enough. It is an unfortunate fact that poems exhibiting dismal rhymes such as these are not only being written, but are being offered for publication or entered in competitions.

If no word which suits your meaning rhymes with your key word, there is nothing to stop you from altering the key word. So instead of saying:

Green buds piercing through the earth

you could say:

Green buds piercing through the soil

lending itself to a follow-up line:

Reward the gardener for his toil

Or you could use:

Green buds piercing through the ground

and follow it with:

Are pledge that flowers will soon abound.

Again, these are not wonderful lines of earth-shattering beauty, but they do demonstrate the widening range of options for the poet who is willing to strive for sensible rhymes.

When you spent some time toying with full rhyme, write some slant-rhymed poetry. You extend your options enormously by considering slant rhyme rather than full. Here you have the opportunity to increase your range of suitably sounding words by accepting any similarity of sound as the binding factor for your poem.

Prove how much wider your choice has become by making lists of words which offer some sound similarity to a key word. See how long these lists are in comparison with the list of full rhymes. Returning to the original example, look at the word 'earth', first considering full rhymes and then the slant-rhyme options.

EARTH – full rhymes

birth, rebirth, unearth, dearth, firth, mirth, worth, girth.

EARTH – slant rhymes

beneath, heath, heather, either, earn, hearth, earthly, oath, terse, worse, earthenware, turn, uncouth, third, heard, loathe, flirt, breath, uncertain . . . etc.

When searching for an appropriate full rhyme, you do have one useful tool at your disposal, in the shape of a rhyming dictionary. Slant rhymes need to spring from your own mind, but because you are seeking only some slight resonance with the key word, where an element of its sound rather than the complete sound is mirrored, the list is vast.

If your poem relies on infrequent examples of slant rhyme, it will not have an appreciable rhyming effect. The more you use, the more insistently slant rhyme will impose its subtle harmonies on your writing.

Administration

It is a good idea to institute a record system to help with your analysis of poetry by other people. Each time you read a poem, whether you are looking at it with a critical eye or simply enjoying a relaxing read, you absorb something of the crafting through which it was forged. This implies that you are accumulating a store of useful information for your own writing. Every idea which delights you, every device which appeals to you, every subtlety of construction or content which makes you think can have an effect on your own work.

It is easy to make these observations at the time of reading, and then to forget all about them. By keeping a careful note of them you will have a wealth of good ideas at your fingertips.

Write down any words or phrases which are new to you or seem to be cleverly fabricated. You are not doing this in order to incorporate the words directly into your own poem, but to find means of expression which are equally powerful or unexpected.

Note the viewpoint from which the poem is expressed. Is it challenging or unusual? Could you imagine the same material retold from a different angle?

Note any interesting factors in the poem's form, its line pattern, stanza construction or its placing on the page. Is there an exciting rhythm, or an unusual use of rhyme?

Return to a wider view of the poem, and look again at its themes and subject matter. Do they open new insights; do they intrigue or puzzle you?

It is even worth noting the titles of poems which you find especially telling or memorable, but whose effectiveness is impossible to define. You can always go back to them in the future to look at them again, and make a fresh attempt at analysis.

By categorising the elements of a poem's effectiveness, you are both fixing it more firmly in your mind and widening your own poetic horizons. An occasional glance through your collected notes will give an instant recharge to an output which is becoming predictable or jaded.

Fun

It is easy to hold the past masters of poetry in awe. It is worth

taking an occasional appreciative, but irreverent, look at
their work. You can have a kindly laugh at their expense,
and, at the same time, exercise your mind on their writing.

Some of the elements of this game are akin to the writing
of parodies, but here the idea is not to emulate the style of a
selected poet, but to add to one of his works.

You can recreate the splendours of *Kubla Khan* by beefing
up Coleridge's fragment. You can write your own comments
on any great poem of your choice. You can substitute a stanza of your own for one of the master's.

For example, think about *Daffodils*, probably the best
known of Wordsworth's poems. The version we know reads:

> I wandered lonely as a cloud
>   That floats on high o'er vales and hills,
> When all at once I saw a crowd,
>   A host, of golden daffodils;
> Beside the lake, beneath the trees,
> Fluttering and dancing in the breeze.
>
> Continuous as the stars that shine
>   And twinkle on the Milky Way,
> They stretched in never-ending line
>   Along the margin of a bay;
> Ten thousand saw I at a glance,
> Tossing their heads in sprightly dance.
>
> The waves beside them danced, but they
>   Out-did the sparkling waves in glee:
> A poet could not but be gay,
>   In such a jocund company:
> I gazed – and gazed – but little thought
> What wealth the show to me had brought:
>
> For oft, when on my couch I lie
>   In vacant or in pensive mood,
> They flash upon that inward eye

Which is the bliss of solitude;
And then my heart with pleasure fills,
And dances with the daffodils.

It is a simple matter to bring this material up to date by
adding a stanza reflecting a 'popular' view of poetry, e.g.:

Now when examinations loom
  And schoolboys have to study rhyme,
And lower third is filled with gloom,
  There is one consolation: time
Will pass and free them from their lot –
And poetry can go and rot.

Or you can debase the poem by taking its most famous lines
and fitting your own highly unsuitable words to them, e.g:

I wandered lonely as a cloud –
  B.O. disperses any crowd.

Or:

I wandered lonely as a cloud
  That floats on high o'er vales and hills,
For triple whiskies had allowed
  No memory of bar-room bills.

Or:

For oft, when on my couch I lie
  In vacant or in pensive mood,

I note I can no longer spy
My feet, and curse my love of food.

There is no commercial value in this exercise, nor does it achieve any spectacular results in terms of increased skills. It does, however, induce you to play with words and play with poetry – essential for the serious writer, regardless of the whimsical form the play takes.

Form

The ballade, like the ode, can take various forms. In this most common pattern, it consists of three stanzas of eight lines each, and an envoi of four lines offering a final comment or note of explanation. The lines are usually written in iambic pentameter or iambic tetrameter.

A refrain line closes each stanza and the envoi, and this refrain should move the poem forward with each repetition.

There are only three rhymes used throughout, in a pattern of:

a b a b b c b C   a b a b b c b C   a b a b b c b C   b c b C

Example: *Beware Mermaids*

I dug my bare toes into sand	a
and watched and waited fall of night	b
while shadows lengthened on the land	a
and sky shed coloured threads of light.	b
Clouds greyed to purple in the height	b
as darkness gathered over me.	c
Sun blazed last fire, then slipped from sight	b
into the cold embrace of sea.	C

With black came silence to the strand.	a
I felt a shivering of fright,	b
but stayed, unmoving, for I planned	a
to catch a glimpse of water sprite.	b
I knew from ancient lore I might	b
find mermaids sitting by the quay,	c
and diving, silvered in moonlight,	b
into the cold embrace of sea.	C
My wish was granted. As I scanned	a
the harbourside and waves, a bright	b
gold head appeared, then more, a band	a
of nymphs who sported in delight,	b
flashed tails of sparkling malachite,	b
sang out strange music luring me	c
by unseen force of boundless might	b
into the cold embrace of sea.	C
I struggled to resist, to fight,	b
turn back on looming fate and flee –	c
but mystic song dragged me from flight	b
into the cold embrace of sea.	C

This is one version of the form, which originated in France. There are several set variants of it, and scope for the imaginative writer to devise his own.

The tightness of rhyme and the sense of control imposed by the line structure gives this form a taut, dynamic appeal which works with a wide range of subjects.

Workshop

There are times when the initial idea for a poem will present itself in a particular form, and others when the poem cries out for an individual but highly disciplined pattern which resembles no form you know. On these latter occasions, it is a stimulating exercise to create your own form, guided by the poem you are writing.

There is no such thing as formless poetry. The first appearance of words on paper assumes a shape. While the words are flowing in your mind, pour them down on to paper as quickly as you can. You may end up with mere notes, or with the first draft of a poem. Wait until the words stop flowing before you look too carefully at your writing.

First consider its shape on the page. Are you writing a long or a short poem? Are the lines brief or lengthy? Have your notes divided themselves – without conscious thought from you, perhaps – into a pattern of stanzas?

The final version of the poem may look nothing like this draft, but now that there is some pattern appearing on the paper, you are beginning to develop a form around which you can work.

Look at the relationship between your subject matter and the pattern, trusting your instinct to marry theme and form. Remember that all the poetry you have read is supporting your instinct in this medium: your experience of poetry will guide you in the right direction.

Look more carefully at the pattern of alignment which is building up in your poem. Are you happy with it? Is there a natural movement through the lines of each stanza? Be prepared to experiment if the line pattern does not quite fit.

As always in the creation of poetry, reading aloud will help you to assess your writing. Listen to the metre emerging in the lines, and to the subtleties of rhythm. Listen for any elements of rhyme which are there.

As you tune in to these facets of your poem you can start to think about imposing them, rather than simply letting them happen. If the poem leans toward an iambic metre, focus on this and strive to create iambic lines. If it shows evidence of slant-rhymed couplets, seek out sound similarities as you write each pair of lines. Throughout the process, check continually to ensure that you are creating the best possible vehicle to convey your ideas.

The more you draw the different aspects of your poem together, the more firmly a pattern will emerge. Study it with care. Does it resemble any established form? If so, your poem may be a new variation on that pattern. Is it unique? You may have achieved the distinction of creating an entirely new form.

Whether you have produced an original pattern or a variant, the next stage is to develop it. Exploit your ideas, and write frequently in your form. At best, it could become an accepted vehicle for poetry. At worst, you have created an exciting device for your own personal use.

Exercises

1   Take an apple, or another piece of fruit. Examine it, using all of your senses. Cut it and eat some. Write notes, and then produce a highly detailed poem in any form based on the experience.

2   For ten minutes, allow yourself the indulgence of playing about with words and their meanings. Devise cryptic clues for single words or short phrases, as if you were preparing them for a crossword puzzle.

3   Go back to the notes you wrote in exercise 1. Use them as the basis for a poem on any subject except fruit.

DAY NINE

Reading

Read some work by any poet for whom richness of language was/is a way of life (e.g. Dylan Thomas, Gerard Manley Hopkins). Although it is good advice to opt for the plainest, most ordinary words to express your thoughts in poetry, there is always the exceptional occasion when you will want to use something richer and fuller. By reading poets whose major output falls into this category, you will become totally familiar with the techniques you need to apply.

Read silently and then aloud, noting the different effect the poem has on you in the printed and the voiced medium. Ask yourself whether the poem relies on mellifluent words, or more mundane words put into a fluently harmonious order.

Consider the poem's subject matter. Is there anything in it which lends itself to a highly poetic approach? Imagine the same subject matter in the hands of any other writer of your choice. How would the style differ from the example before you?

Look at the metre of the poem, its rhythm and rhyme. Do they contribute to the quality of richness?

Being totally honest in your answer, ask whether the message of the poem is submerged by the verbosity of its medium. Does the rounded use of language swamp all meaning?

Look at the proportion of adjectives and adverbs in the poem. Is it higher than that of your own poetry? Is it higher or lower than you expected?

Write down a few of the poet's lines in ordinary conversational language. Now, without referring to the text, try another version using your own idiom and style. Still resisting the temptation to look again at the original, attempt to emulate it, recreating the poet's lines in an approximation of his version.

Examine your three versions of the lines alongside the poet's originals. Which of the four do you like best? Which communicates most clearly? Which uses language most richly?

Take the wide view once again, asking yourself the root question of poetry appreciation. Do you like the poem? If so why? If not, why not? In giving your answers you are offering indications of the style you most like to read, which is likely to affect the style in which you write.

Compare your 'richness' reading with the poetry of a writer who uses a much more stark, spare form of expression. Which holds more appeal for you? Which is nearer in construction to your own writing?

Writing

Write your own poem which relies for its effect on the rich use of language. Start with some detailed notes, painting the most vivid pictures you can of your observations, however exciting or ordinary they might be.

Focus on tiny areas of your notes, rather than looking at your theme as a whole. Try out different means of expressing these areas. While you are doing this, concentrate on using language as fully and richly as you can. You may end up with a list of half-a-dozen phrases which say the same thing but in different ways.

Put the list on one side while you explore a new area of the notes, and repeat the process. When you have put each area under a literary microscope in this way, you should have a network of alternative expressions in a jumble. They are unlikely to bear any resemblance to a complete poem at this stage.

Read all of the expressions on the page, and then speak

them aloud. Somewhere during this process the perfect means of conveying your message should reveal itself to you. If this happens, proceed to the next stage. If it does not, put all your notes away for a while – an hour, a few days, a week – before reading them through once again. Repeat the exercise as many times as you need to, until your language route through the poem becomes clear.

The next stage is to draw the separate phrases together into the form of a poem. In theory this should be a simple task. You have already worked your way through the alternatives of vocabulary and expression, and are only seeking to make a harmonious whole. The 'only' is not necessarily so easy. You have, in a sense, dissected the poem before it was written. Putting it together is not quite the same as doing a jigsaw. It involves the creation of a work of art, not a mere mechanical function.

You may find it useful to highlight areas of your notes with a marker pen and read them in isolation. You may find it easier to keep all the notes together, so that you can 'mix and match' the expressions while you work through them.

Having sought out the richest expressions you could find for this raw material, it is logical that the whole poem will have a strongly poetic effect. Be sensitive to the developing aura of the poem, ensuring that richness is never allowed to degenerate either into sentimentality or into an egotistical display of cleverness.

At the same time, let your fertile mind take those leaps of the imagination which will make your poem transcend the expected. Wallow in richness, but be sure your poem does not drown in it.

Administration

In the chaotic world of writing poetry, it is a good idea to devise an aims and achievements plan. This helps you with the disciplines of writing. It may seem contradictory to talk about discipline in the context of a creative medium; but the fact that writing poetry may be a spasmodic task undertaken irregularly and not scheduled into any timetable means that ordering the activity is all the more important. If you want to be a poet, you have to write poetry, and if you have some direction and ambition in your writing, you will probably write more effectively.

Beginning with the aims, you can start with the vaguest of intentions. You might make a list which reads:

- increased output
- publication in a wider range of magazines
- publicising myself as a poet
- preparing a collection of 50–60 poems.

Depending on how organised you like to be, you might then qualify the suggestions on the list with further details, e.g.:

- increased output through setting aside an additional two hours per week for writing, and keeping thorough notes of all embryonic ideas so that writing time is used most effectively
- publication in more magazines by keeping to a regular programme of submissions, aiming to have at least four batches of poetry entered with publications at any one time, and by seeking out magazines which are new to me
- publicising myself by giving notice of writing achievements to local press and radio, suggesting poetry coverage in local press (e.g. a 'Poets' Corner', poetry competition, etc.) and registering with the local reference library/arts centre my willingness to give poetry readings
- aiming for publication of my collection within the next 12 months, deciding on my preferred method of publication and gaining information about it, compiling a file of suitable work

At this stage it is useful to look at the other part of the plan, and make an achievements list. Decide on a timescale for your achievements. You might register all of your successes gained during the past six months, or since the beginning of the year. Categorise your achievements under appropriate headings, e.g. completed poems, acceptances, competition awards.

Keep the lists beside you, and remember to bring them up to date at regular intervals. In a world which has its share of rejections and disappearances-without-trace, it is not self-absorbed but sensible to hold the positive in sight. Revel in your achievements. They are the spur to future successes.

Return to thoughts of your aims, and work out a specific programme of writing intentions for the next week or month. List the poems-in-progress on which you want to work. Allocate set times of day when you will be available to write. Plan any submissions you intend to make, and leave the lion's share of your time for the vital part of the task – the creation of poetry.

Remember to build into your programme leeway for either of the two imponderables. Allow yourself the flexibility to deviate from the programme the moment inspiration strikes, and you feel that you must put a poem on to paper. Be gentle enough with yourself to accept that there are days when the writing will not flow, and no amount of discipline will compensate for the absence of any germ of creativity. Be prepared to go away and do something entirely different, secure in the knowledge that you are permitting yourself a fallow period, letting your mind range over other things to refresh itself before returning to your writing. Reschedule your next writing session, and relax sufficiently to look forward to it.

While you can design a plan for your writing life in a matter of minutes, its effectiveness can only be judged over a prolonged period of time. By streamlining your plan with experience, you will devise your own most useful approach to writing poetry, and make the best possible use of your time.

Fun

Acrostics are a diverting form of poetry, allowing you to write a 'concealed' message literally alongside your poem.

The first letter of each line, when read downwards, spells out a name or message.

Acrostics can be written in any form, but traditionally they use rhyme and metre. Start by spelling your message down the side of the page, and then complete the lines in a way which creates a poem, or even a silly rhyme, e.g.:

A nyone can write a verse –
L ines like these are somewhat terse,
I nsisting on a form of rhyme
S ome find dismal, some sublime.
O ne blessing, though, attends this sport –
N o epic, this. It's very short.

Although the rhymed, metrical form is a convention, there is no reason why you should not write in free verse, e.g.:

A rachnoid shiver-touches
L eave tracks of fright, form
I ndigo shadows latticed across
S kin. Jaws taut, I try to think
O f petal brush, caress of lover –
N othing numbs the fear.

If your message has more than one word, you can start a new stanza for each word, or write in a continuous block.

You may prefer to place your message on the right-hand side of your page, by writing a telestich. In this, the letters at the ends of the lines spell out your message, instead of those at the line beginnings. If the puzzle factor fascinates you, try a double acrostic, where the last letter of each line is the same as the first. This produces an identical message down the line ends. Add to your message by creating a compound acrostic. The first letters of the lines spell out a message, the last letters an entirely different one.

The most important part of this exercise is the ludic element, where word play enhances your skills in manipulating words. It is an added bonus if you manage to create a good poem at the same time.

Form

Alcaic quatrains originated as a Greek form. They are unrhymed, depending on a strict metrical pattern to provide a poetic unity.

The first foot of each of the first three lines is an acephalous iambus, i.e. an iambus which has shed its first syllable to produce a single, stressed syllable.

Lines one and two take the same metrical pattern. After the acephalous iambus, each consists of two trochees and then two dactyls. The third line takes four trochees after the initial syllable. The fourth, lacking a first acephalous foot, consists of two dactyls followed by two trochees.

Where x indicates an unstressed and / a stressed syllable, the quatrain pattern reads:

```
/    / x    / x   / x x    / x x
/    / x    / x   / x x    / x x
/    / x    / x   / x    / x
/ x x    / x x    / x    / x
```

This looks as confusing as it sounds. In practice, it is not a difficult pattern to create once you have absorbed its distinctive rhythm.

Look at the following example, comparing its feet with those indicated above. Say it aloud to appreciate the sound values created by this form.

Example: *Night Walk: Sorrento*

Day lingers here, with sun beating hard on us,
bright sky Madonna blue as at noon. There is

dust; hum of saws. The men are cutting
magic from wood for the eager tourists.

Walk further. Leave the resinous odours, and
breathe deeply from the air by the esplanade.
Watch water, oil warm, slide on black sand,
fishing boats bobbing and busy ferries.

See bats dart, cleaving dusk as the sun starts to
dip, falling into water and darkening
dusk. Stripes of red and orange flicker,
changing to purple as night takes over.

Now from the cloistered quadrangle, music to
haunt dreams, to fill our waking with wonderment
plays, filters through the air. The pious
brothers are drawn from their prayers to listen.

Shops flaunt their wares to crowds blocking alleyways,
all bright with welcome, urging the visitors,
whose wallets bulge with lire for the
gifts to remind them of so much magic.

Walk past the baker's, tasting the freshly made
loaves in anticipation of morning, and
feel velvet warmth of night whose blackness,
full now and deep, shades the late hour backdrop.

Leave now the colour, noise and the crowds, and take
roads leading back to silence, our place where the
love forged between us makes complete the
circle of truth with each arc a promise.

In common with other forms of poetry which rely on the
metrical pattern rather than rhyming sounds to create their
effect, the alcaic quatrain appears to have few of the elements
of poetry inherent in it when heard as an isolated stanza. The

example given here offers seven stanzas, which should repeat the pattern sufficiently to establish itself.

Workshop

Having considered writing rhymed poetry in Day Eight, it is worth thinking about the manner of introducing rhyme into your poems, and the point in their construction when decisions have to be taken.

Sometimes there is no choice to be made. The idea for the poem presents itself in the rhyming format which is right for it. You do not even ask yourself the question, 'Should I use rhyme?' You start to write, and the emerging poem sets itself into lines, and tells you if and when it needs rhyming sounds.

The problems arise with those ideas which do not come as part of a package. In theory, the best course of action would be to attempt the first few lines of the poem in a variety of different rhyme styles. Try using free verse, full rhyme, slant rhyme, different combinations of rhyming and metrical patterns, and sooner or later one will assert itself as the best form for your poem. Then go on to write the poem.

In practice, it is a little different. The first outpouring of words on to paper should be allowed to flow unhampered. This is when the poem's dynamics form themselves, when the touch of magic is injected into the words. It is all very well to revise the poem later, but the initial part of the craft should be totally creative, saving the technical back-up work until the first draft is all on paper, or for another occasion.

The trouble with following this latter course is that if your initial choice in the use of rhyme is the wrong one, it is incredibly difficult to revise the poem with such radical alterations. It may be that the only course open to you is to rewrite the poem, but this inevitably means that you lose the spontaneity and excitement of the first draft.

There is no blanket answer to the problem. Experiment to discover which approach works best for you, and then either stick to one method of finding your way in rhyme, or adapt the method to suit the individual poem. My own preference is to pour the poem out, whether or not the rhyming device works. If I am dissatisfied, I produce another, different poem on the same theme rather than a complete rewrite of the flawed poem.

This is a hit-and-miss approach, but there is one simple exercise you can practise which gives a good insight into the whole question of rhyme choice.

Take any poem you like, written by anybody. The one limitation is that, if you choose one of your own poems, it should be one you feel was finished months or even years ago. If your selected poem is written in full rhyme, rewrite it removing all vestiges of rhyme, to produce a free verse poem. Then look for other options which would offer slant rhymes rather than full. If the original is a free verse poem, rewrite it with rhyme, again trying full and slant rhyme.

Compare the versions to see which pleases you most, and which is the best vehicle for conveying the poem's message.

This is no more than an exercise, but it gives you an object lesson in the dynamics of rhyme within poetry. Through practice of this sort, you will develop your own instincts so that they will guide you accurately through rhyme choice when you write.

Exercises

1   Imagine a box of any sort, shape and size. Write a poem about whatever is in it.
2   Browse through any set of instructions, e.g. directions for working a household appliance, a recipe, knitting pattern etc. Look for any found poems – i.e. unconsciously poetic lines and phrases, which occur by chance in prosaic material. See whether you can work them into an acceptable poem.
3   Write a poem from the negative viewpoint of one of your fears, or the positive viewpoint of one of your fantasies.

DAY TEN

Reading

Take any book of contemporary poetry, a single-author collection or an anthology of work by different people. Read as much of it as you can take in. Read quickly, and not selectively. The aim of this exercise is to swamp yourself in the writing of today.

When you have read in a concentrated fashion for half-an-hour or so, go away and do something completely different for a little while. Come back to your book, and have another look at the same poems.

This time be more selective with your reading. Skip over any poem which had no effect on you the first time you read it. Only reread those poems which held some attraction. Spend more time on the poems which intrigue you, whether or not you like their subjects, and less on the ones with surface appeal.

Analyse your reactions to the poems which are allowed a second reading. Do you view them with pleasure, repugnance, envy? ('I wish I'd written that' is the most complimentary remark a poet can hear.) Do you want to return to them, or do they insist on attracting your attention, possibly against your will? Are there common themes and subjects? If so, do they have any special relevance for you?

Now consider the technicalities of these poems. Are they all in free verse, strict form, a combination? Do they have exciting use of language in common? Are they, for the most part, written in the forms you prefer for your own writing, or do they bear no technical resemblance to your poems?

Put them aside again for a while. Before you go back to them, try to remember titles, themes and subjects you found in them. Jot down any telling lines or phrases which have remained in your memory. Test your memory against the poems, rediscovering the points of effectiveness.

The purpose in this reading exercise is two-fold. The benefits of reading poetry should never be underestimated by a poet. The immersion of oneself in the poetry of today is the easiest way to snap into creative mode. But there is the second point. The poems you have been reading have all been published. Even the ones which you did not consider worthy of a second glance have appealed to an editor. By discovering the root of that appeal, you are halfway to making your own poetry fit into acceptable patterns, or at least to refining the selection process which guides you to submit particular poems to certain outlets.

Writing

Concentrate on producing some poetry which really releases an intensity of emotion. This means shedding all your inhibitions and, in a poetic sense, drawing attention to yourself. It means forgetting the reserve which many of us feel about opening up poetically, and speaking out frankly and eloquently about our deepest feelings.

You do not have to select highly emotive subject matter about which to write. The ordinary concerns of life can give rise to profound emotional reactions. It is easy to gloss over emotions and merely describe episodes. If you do this, you are creating a two-dimensional version of the theme of your poem. Whether or not you admit the fact to yourself, you are holding back a part of the full experience which will leave you with vague feelings of dissatisfaction about your writing. The reader will be able to sense this reticence, and feel cheated.

It is perhaps easier to practise the technique of letting go emotionally on ordinary subjects. You feel less self-conscious about expressing strong feelings if the context is one of every-day concern. Throughout your writing, examine every stirring reaction to your subject matter. Explore it fully, allowing yourself to delve deeply and report explicitly on your reactions.

Keep reminding yourself that your poem, at this stage, is for your eyes only. If you find that your material is 'over the top', and genuinely feel that you would be ashamed to have anyone else read it, all you have to do is rewrite it. There is no need for embarrassment. Your poem remains between you and your notebook.

Before you delete it, however, take a careful look at the emotional content of your poem. Is your reaction well founded, or are you merely responding with surprise to a style which transcends your usual writing? Be sure that you are not making your poem bland by dropping its more passionate areas.

It is rather more difficult to assess the effectiveness of your emotional writing when your subject matter is highly charged. A poem which deals with powerful feelings must dig deeply into emotional responses. The best guide to the acceptability of your writing is to question your sincerity. If you have written with fidelity to the experience and minute attention to the detail with which you have described it, you should have no problem. As soon as you try to force emotional reactions which are incompatible with the experience, the poem begins to founder.

Remember that genuine reactions may be transferred into different areas of subject matter. It is not always necessary to marry reactions with the true circumstances which provoked them; by using your imagination you will be able to adapt conditions and experiment by applying known responses to appropriate areas.

Although an emotional release is therapeutic for you and adds an extra dimension of enjoyment for your reader, do not forget that poetry can degenerate into sentimentality all too easily. Be careful not to fall into the trap of using cheap emotionalism as a substitute for accurate and considered portrayals of sensations. Above all, think in terms of balance. There is a delicate balance to be achieved between sentiment and sentimentality, emotion and emotionalism. If you are ever in doubt, put your writing away for a while before reassessing its content. If you remain in doubt, remember that it is better to delete an entire poem than allow your name to appear on a text relying on false sentiment or thoughts.

Administration

While market study is essential for the poet hoping to place work for publication, it should not be forgotten that new markets can be made. It is a useful project to spend a little time trying to find a new niche for poetry, and being sure you are in a position to provide material for that niche.

Special interest magazines devoted to computers, hot air ballooning, crochet, zoology, etc. may be pleased to feature poems. Have you ever submitted poetry based on their special interest to them? If they do not publish poetry, have you thought of approaching them suggesting that they might use poems?

Some publications state clearly in the annual writers' handbooks that they have no interest in poetry. Fair enough; but if poetry is not mentioned at all, why not try to create a new outlet for yourself and fellow poets? A brief telephone call or businesslike letter making the suggestion might open up a whole new area of writing on the appropriate subject.

If you find a new outlet in this way, remember that for general readers who do not normally enjoy reading poetry, rhymed, metrical, traditional forms are most accessible. Free verse has to be constructed with great care to make sure that it communicates directly.

This idea does not only apply to specialist magazines available on the newsagent's shelf. Approach the wide range of trade magazines in the same way.

General interest magazines occasionally print poems or readers' letters on the editorial pages, or feature them in a box to break up a bulk of text. Make sure that you take advantage of outlets which already exist before approaching other editors with the suggestion that poetry might be included.

Local and national newspapers are another potential source of publication. On a smaller (and usually non-paying) scale, there are local community and parish magazines plus club newsletters all over the country. Publication there would enhance your status as a writer in the neighbourhood.

Casting your net more widely, look for outlets in your locality where a one-off poem or series of poems would add an extra dimension to some other facet of local life. If you are interested in writing poetry based on paintings, approach your art gallery to see whether poems could be displayed alongside pictures, or published in a book with pictures of the paintings they illustrate. The same approach could be used with museums and libraries, where poems shedding further light on the exhibits/books could be put on show.

Do not restrict your search for outlets to places in the public domain. Look at commercial concerns. Could you produce poems for restaurant menus, about local pubs, or to help advertise hotels in your town? Are there any shops which would be interested in displaying poems relating to the items they sell?

You might care to write poetry to highlight the concerns of a local charity, for use in your neighbourhood schools, to describe the animals in your nearest zoo ... the possibilities are limitless.

Few of these suggested outlets will bring you financial returns; but this is nothing new to a poet. Besides, you need to create opportunities. You are heightening public awareness in poetry along with your reputation as a poet. Make your own list of subjects about which you would like to write, and places where such writing might be appreciated. Work through your lists, keeping records of all your approaches and their results. You may be surprised by the success of your venture.

Fun

Do you have a funny tale to tell? Write it in the form of a verse monologue in rhyming couplets. This is an excellent vehicle for a witty story. A tripping rhythm and the predictability of paired line rhymes will contribute to the humour.

A verse monologue differs from a rhymed joke, in that it relates a story which should be amusing throughout, rather than giving information which only becomes funny when you reach the punchline.

The best material for monologues is often rooted in truth. Actual events may be no more than the spark of the idea, and exaggerations and fabrications take over when the fund of authentic material runs out. Stretch your poetic licence as far as you wish in order to create a good story. Just as you might embroider a sequence of genuine events for dramatic effect, expand within your monologue to get the most laughs from it.

If you cannot think of any real events on which to build, there is nothing wrong with using your imagination. Again, if your own ideas refuse to flow, crib the basic circumstances – but no more than these – from a humorous book or TV series.

Your 'cribbing' should be restricted to a situation. Perhaps your source material is an excerpt from a book where a number of characters go on a disaster-ridden picnic. Limit your stealing to the idea of a picnic where things go wrong – and make them different from the blunders in the original. You might be basing your idea on a situation comedy about a family going through a series of traumas with two teenage daughters. Adapt your monologue to treat, say, the tribulations of raising teenage boys, and you will have created a distance from your source material.

Having come up with the circumstances that will offer you a range of humorous opportunities, you must be sure to keep the momentum throughout your writing. There should be a new source of amusement at least once every six lines, or your material will become tedious and, possibly, too descriptive.

In addition to keeping up your flow of witty input, check

continuously to make sure that your rhyme and metre are applied with precision. Part of the fun of this sort of writing is its strict adherence to the expected pattern. Deviate from it to the slightest degree, and you may have weakened your writing. The exception to this rule is the occasional poem whose form is deliberately subverted for comic effect, e.g. in a limerick which leads the reader to expect a bawdy final word then substitutes something non-rhyming and innocuous.

Although your monologue needs to be funny throughout, it is a good idea to have a strong punchline to which you can work. Build up the humour, circumstance on circumstance, towards a climax which is the 'belly laugh' of the whole piece. Then bring your poem to a speedy conclusion.

The suggestion is to write in rhyming couplets, but monologues can work perfectly well in other forms. Do remember, though, that a strict pattern of rhyme and metre applied throughout will reinforce the humour of your writing.

Comic styles of writing are best suited to performance. Work can be enjoyed from the page, but part of the fun is an appropriate and tripping delivery. Whoever is going to read your work aloud should practise until it can be delivered with wit and panache.

Form

The terzanelle could be described as a cross between a terza rima and a villanelle. It is one of those forms which appears to be incredibly complicated until you get into the swing of writing it, when it all falls into place quite simply.

As in both of its parent forms, the bulk of the poem is written in tercets. The completed piece is nineteen lines long. It is usually loosely based on an iambic metre of four or five feet, but it seems to work most effectively with a freer metre than either of its parents.

The chain-rhymed scheme consists of two lines which rhyme on either side of the line whose rhyme is carried into the next stanza. This line rhymes with the first line of the next stanza, and is repeated as its final line. The middle line of this stanza is carried into the next, and the process repeated.

Five tercets are produced in this way, and the poem ends with a quatrain, which offers an option. Its second and third lines may be a repeat of the opening line of the poem followed by the repeated middle line of the final tercet, or the repeated middle line of the final tercet followed by the repeated opening line of the poem. The tercet rhyme pattern is:

A1 B A2 b C B c D C d E D e F E

followed by the quatrain consisting of:

f A1 or F F or A1 A2

It is probably easier to appreciate these points in an example.

Example: *Point of Contact*

When I cannot find my place	A1
within the universe inside my head	B
I reach across and touch your face.	A2
Your warm flesh shocks my fingers. Dread	b
subsides in tangible belief	C
within the universe inside my head.	B
This comfort is my sole relief,	c
for torture of unknowing fear	D
subsides in tangible belief	C
Where I can look up and see you near.	d
You are the only help I need	E
for torture of unknowing fear.	D
If I am faced with torment, squalor, greed,	e
no terrors can disperson me.	F
You are the only help I need.	E

When I forget who I should be,	f
when I cannot find my place,	A1
no terrors can disperson me;	F
I reach across and touch your face.	A2

This form is not the easiest to produce, but offers a most attractive option if neither of its parent forms quite fits your subject matter. If you can, try to move the poem forward with each repetition you include. A terzanelle can be produced with strict metre, but metrical flexibility gives it a delightfully free 'feel'.

Workshop

Look back at the poetry you have written, and ask yourself which of it is truly memorable. No matter how good a poem may be, it must have the quality of compulsion to make its greatest effect. It must remain with its reader long after the book has been closed.

It is difficult to assess your own poetry in this capacity. You are unlikely to forget one of your own creations, and if it slips from your mind for a while, your memory is jogged the moment you look at it again. You have to try to stand back from the poem and ask yourself which elements of it are most likely to stay with a reader.

The most obviously memorable factor is the subject matter. A poem dealing with an unusual subject, or one which offers some new insight, has built-in memorability. When checking through your poems, look for this factor first. Any poem which satisfies these criteria is approaching the elusive originality which will make it memorable.

If there is any gimmicky aspect of the poem that, too, will make it memorable. If, for example, you have conveyed your message in the form of a dialogue, or created an interesting visual pattern on the page, your work has a better chance of remaining in the mind.

Strong titles and unexpected forms are another good indication, and the stimulus of a challenge or some radical idea will also help.

Checking for memorability is a little like gross revision. The attention is not focused on to every facet of the text, but the overall effect of the poem is being assessed and reassessed.

It is a good idea to keep a list of those poems which you feel are especially memorable. They may be competition pieces, or at least be ready for publication. Those poems which fail to make the list should be scrutinised once again. You might find that this exercise helps to weed out the inadequate as well as pinpointing your strongest work.

One word of warning. Do not be too harsh in your evaluations. It is easy, at a time when your ideas are not flowing and your self-esteem is flagging, to denigrate all of your writing. You are looking for honesty and self-awareness, not trying to put every poem you have written on to the rack.

Exercises

1   Write a list of ten adjectives. Add to each the noun which you feel fits most obviously with it (e.g. grassy + meadow, fierce + lion). Now change your combinations around, so that you end up with the least likely descriptions with the nouns (e.g. fierce meadow, grassy lion). Does anything inspire you to produce a poem? Incorporate as many of the 'twisted' combinations as you wish. You may find that your poem dispenses with the need for adjectives, which can then be jettisoned.

2   Write a poem in any form, based on a bird.

3   Address a poem to any person of your choice, alive or dead. (NB If you are aiming for publication, and the person is alive, make sure that your poem is not libellous!)

DAY ELEVEN

Reading

Look at the work of any poet laureate. You may choose one of the great names who has held this position, or somebody whose work is comparatively unknown. Whatever your opinion of the poetry, you are looking at writing which, in its time, was held in particular esteem.

Read through a few poems, giving yourself an overview of the writer's work. Think about the impetus prompting the poet to produce them. Do they have a spontaneous air, or do they seem forced? Is the subject matter unusual or outstanding? Are the themes light or heavyweight?

If the appointment of poet laureate had been in your gift, would you have chosen the same person? Can you predict who will succeed the present poet laureate in that position?

Now return to the poetry and focus on one or two pieces. Ask yourself whether your selected poems have any special features, or stand out in any way from the bulk of poetry being written at the time.

While it is impossible to build up a clear picture of a poet from such a tiny sample of his output, the focusing on just a couple of poems allows you to scrutinise each one carefully.

Take your target poems apart, from an artistic and technical viewpoint. Spend as much time on them as your own poetic instincts suggest. Analyse each aspect of their construction, examining motivation, handling of material, balance, rhyming, rhythm, metrical devices, use of language, etc. Do this on a comparative level. How does each aspect of the poem compare with your own preferred means of handling the same facet of your own writing?

This comparison is not being made to encourage you to produce a pastiche of the target work. It is done to satisfy a poet's natural curiosity about the way in which a fellow poet has tackled the same questions which affect you.

It is easy to lose sight of the fact that all poets go through a common experience. The searching for a word, the striving to make a message plain, the agony of cutting for the developing strength of a poem are part of the job. From ancient times to the end of time, poets are faced with these same problems. It does not hurt to remind yourself of that occasionally.

Writing

Every holiday you take, short or long, local or exotic, should provide you with material for producing poetry. During this writing period, use memories of your holidays or notes you made on them to fuel poems.

Think of the journey, with its ever-changing scenery, its sense of movement, sound and rhythm. Each view from the window of a car, train, plane or ship is the cameo of a moment. Recall the most memorable from your last vacation, and examine each for the germ of a poem. Add imagination to memory to spark the flame.

Imagine yourself into 'holiday mode' to experience through memory the total relaxation which is part of a good break. Relax physically. Stretch out on the floor or loll in a chair as restfully as you can. Then think about mental relaxation. Try to empty your mind of everyday concerns. Forget the problems which surround you. Create an illusion of having all the time in the world, and not a care to encroach on it. Allow yourself a good ten minutes in this state.

By the end of your relaxation period, your mind should be teeming with ideas about which you can write. If it is not, try some of these stimuli:

1 Explore three major areas of difference between your most recent holiday venue and your home. Create a series of word pictures, which evoke scenes for you in greater detail than any postcard could.

2 Recall sensory reactions from your last holiday which differed from those you experience at home. How did the unaccustomed sun feel on your skin? How did the sounds you heard in the countryside differ from those you know in town, or vice versa? Precisely what is paella supposed to taste like? Make detailed notes.

3 Read up a little information about the location of a holiday you have enjoyed. Is there scope for a piece of factual poetry about the place?

4 Remember any local tales you heard while you were away, or local customs you observed. Expand on them to produce a poem.

5 If you brought any home, look out your holiday souvenirs. The shells, handmade lace, theatre tickets or rough wine may stimulate you to write.

Having written up this clearly defined, direct material, move away from the immediacy of the experience. Think back through your holiday memories. From this distance, which of your reminiscences is the strongest? What are the emotional responses you recall? Do any characters, incidents or ideas rooted in your holiday clamour to be treated in a poem?

Look through your holiday snapshots. As you remember each occasion which prompted you to take a picture, try to recall the sensations you felt at the time. Were you hot, cold, weary, fresh, hungry, ill, tired? Record these sensations in poetry prompted by the photographs.

As a final thought, resolve to take a special poetry notebook with you the next time you go away, and keep the most thorough notes you can for your future writing. They will provide you with a rich source of material long after the tan has faded.

Administration

If your interest in poetry is serious, you will probably be a subscriber to a number of different poetry magazines. It is a good idea to keep the record of all those you study for use when planning your submissions.

Reading each magazine is the easiest way to familiarise yourself with its editor's requirements, but it is a good idea to keep notes of your own opinion of the poems selected for publication. Your observations may deal in technicalities of construction or apparent preferences in subject matter. If an editor always prints free verse, he is unlikely to appreciate your strict form poetry. If he never uses a poem with any reference to religious matters, he will not change his policy for you.

Keep a correct, up-to-date record of the magazine name, the editor's name and the editorial address alongside your observations. This will save you the time and trouble of looking things up in directories when you are making a submission.

Record details of any special style of submission suggested by the editor. It goes without saying that he will want work to be typed on A4 paper with s.a.e., but he might request two copies of each poem, or a maximum number of poems per submission, a time lapse between submissions, or a line limit per poem. If all this information is readily available to you, you will be able to make the most appropriate submission without having to check through all your back copies of the magazine.

As your experience of each magazine grows, add information such as the average number of weeks it takes for you to receive a 'verdict' on your poetry, and the promptness or otherwise of publication of the magazine.

Make notes about those areas of the magazine which do not include the poems themselves, but offer reviews, editorial material, helpful features, news of competitions or other publications etc. The more information you have about the magazine, the better your chances of finding a niche for your writing in its pages.

Magazine editors are often invited to adjudicate competitions. Use a cross-reference system to reinforce the information in your dossier of adjudicators' preferences. There is nothing wrong with giving yourself an edge over other competitors.

Look at the practical concern of finances. It is a good idea to keep a record of the rising subscription costs and of the payment, if any, you receive for your poetry from each magazine. It is a sad fact that it would be impractical to subscribe to every poetry magazine published; but it makes sense to ensure that your selected subscriptions are providing good value for money.

You might care to consider a scheme which broadens your reading horizons without breaking the bank. There might be another poet near you you who would be willing to share subscription costs, so doubling the number of magazines to which you have access. Check out the possibility of subscribing to an organisation which will provide you with a different magazine every few weeks, such as the Oriel Bookshop, The Friary, Cardiff.

It is surprising how quickly the memory fades and how difficult it can be to remember which article/poem/review appeared in which magazine. By taking a little time to keep market study records, you will have this information at your fingertips.

Fun

Start a poetry diary. Write, in poetry of any form, rhymed or free, metrical or not, details of the highlights of the past week. These may appear as one long poem, or as a sequence of pieces. A sequence may use the same style throughout, or vary in style depending on the subject matter of each of its areas.

This is not just a project for one day. Try to continue it for a sustained period. Design a timetable which fits in with your working pattern, and write a little each day, or once a week, or once a month. Having designed your timetable, stick to it. The disciplines of the exercise are likely to be as valuable as any other aspect of it.

Although you are disciplining yourself into writing regularly, do not be too strict about the way the diary develops. Let your ideas have their head, and be prepared to treat minute details at one writing session and a huge sweep of events at the next.

Record the important events of your life, such as big family occasions, a new job or other upheaval. Record the small things, too – the time you cut your finger, the non-delivery of your newspaper, spilling a cup of coffee. Each has something to yield poetically, and you may surprise yourself by producing better poetry from the minutiae of life rather than from the grand events.

This is intended to be a personal record rather than a catalogue of world happenings, but you might feel moved to write about any item in the news which stirs an emotional reaction in you. Apart from the cathartic effect of writing out your emotion, you may have struck a seam of material which leads you into all sorts of areas of poetry.

While planning your timetable, fix a date for stopping. If your writing is flowing and you find the diary a stimulating exercise, the stop is no more than a pause to go back over all you have written. It may transpire that this exercise does not work for you, and that each entry is a little more stilted and forced than the last. If this is the case, suspend the diary exercise altogether for the time being. You can always come back to it some time in the future.

Your stopping date should be the first time you look back over your diary entries. Although it is tempting to preface each session's writing with a read through of the work you produced last time, try to resist the temptation. Then when the time arrives for you to look back, you will find all sorts of surprises within your pages.

Look back critically, assessing each area of your diary for its development potential. You might have a series of poems which bear no similarity to each other, all of which are worthy of further work. Or the continuous, lengthy poem to which you have added something every day might have evolved as a fascinating document shedding light on to a time in your life.

Extract from your diary all of those pieces which will stand on their own as poems, and follow the usual revision and development route. You may well be pleased with the results.

This diary technique can be particularly useful for a short period of time which is crammed with events, emotions, meetings and partings, etc. A special visit, the days immediately before and after a family wedding, or the Christmas season are perfect examples of these.

Form

Consider the sestina. This is one of those forms which suit jigsaw puzzlers and crossword addicts as well as poets. It is 39 lines long, consisting of six sestets and an envoi of three lines. It is based on six words which appear as the final words of each line of the poem in a predetermined order. In the envoi, all six words appear, one within and one at the end of each line.

Usually unrhymed, the sestina may be written in any single line length and metre. The order of line end words is:

1	A	19	E
2	B	20	C
3	C	21	B
4	D	22	F
5	E	23	A
6	F	24	D
7	F	25	D
8	A	26	E
9	E	27	A

10 B		28 C	
11 D		29 F	
12 C		30 B	
13 C		31 B	
14 F		32 D	
15 D		33 F	
16 A		34 E	
17 B		35 C	
18 E		36 A	

37 B E
38 D C
39 F A

Example: *Secret*

A woman holds the truth no man can learn	A
that tips the balance of our spinning world.	B
Her secret gives the universe its hope	C
in generations to be born. Her soul	D
is seeded, carried by the fickle moon	E
in time with ocean's ebbing, flowing tide.	F
The final draw of childhood's carefree tide	F
turns girl to woman, forces her to learn	A
that truth she will control. Each passing moon	E
offers a new-dreamed phase to fill her world.	B
Her body's blossoming makes flower of soul,	D
instilling its insistent message – hope.	C
To carry in her heart a gleam of hope	C
transports her through her lifetime's summertide	F
where love erupts to cram her brimming soul	D
and teach the final lesson she must learn.	A
For her love's issue populates the world	B
and dances to the rhythms of the moon.	E

And with each passing quarter of the moon   E
the message that insinuates is hope   C
for better times begetting braver world.   B
A universal prayer exhorts the tide   F
of mindlessness to change, and all to learn   A
renewal through new generations' soul.   D

Inexorable movement of the soul   D
through gold of sunlight, silvered beams of moon,   E
permits by grace of time the chance to learn   A
anticipation heady with its hope   C
that day by day, that tide by passing tide,   F
a sense of peace will infiltrate the world.   B

And every woman who walks in the world   B
can savour deep within her heart and soul   D
the Everywoman knowledge. When her tide   F
has ebbed past furthest reaches of the moon,   E
her lasting blessing is the prayer of hope   C
that those who know will note her ways, and learn.   A

For with each world turn and each arc of moon   B/E
that passes, every soul on earth draws hope   D/C
to free the tide of secret lore, and learn.   F/A

There is a rhymed form of the sestina which may be used, taking two rhymed sounds; but the line-end word order is changed in this case so that a pattern of alternately rhyming lines may be established.

Workshop

It is an engaging exercise to work on poems whose prime medium is the spoken word.

A poem can be equally exciting for the reader who sees it

on a page and the listener who hears its lines spoken aloud. In a sense, all poems are heard pieces, as the mind of the silent reader interprets the words on the page, giving them sound values to assist with comprehension. In addition to the writing techniques you apply to every poem, a spoken piece needs certain qualities to assist in its communication.

It is always a good idea to speak your poem repeatedly during its construction. This is especially important in the case of a poem being written for spoken delivery.

As you write, listen for awkward phrases and overuse of alliteration, which become tongue-twisters for the speaker and are tedious for the audience.

Listen, too, for the positive effects of the sounds produced by your words. Onomatopoeic expressions reinforce your poem's message, and allow the speaker to make good use of vocal variety.

Try to avoid the predictability of the cliché. An audience expecting to hear a familiar phrase will be surprised and pleased to hear a new version of it, and will listen with closer attention for similarly favourable images.

Make sure that poetry destined to be spoken aloud deals in direct material without too many nuances which need to be analysed for full interpretation. Keep your intentions for the poem clear, and your audience will experience a sense of reassurance, knowing that it is being guided by a competent hand. Let your meaning sink in a morass of abstractions, obscurity and confusion, and you will lose the attention of your audience.

You are writing for a medium which cannot acknowledge clever presentation on the page, but will absorb the more theatrical elements of your poem. Poetry lending itself to slight movements or gesture, to a choral presentation or to a dramatised version will have an added attraction.

Be aware of the styles and themes of writing which hold special appeal for an audience. Humour is always popular – everybody likes to laugh, and if you are preparing a full programme of spoken poetry, moments of levity and relaxation are essential to release tensions brought on by concentration.

Remember that rhymed or metrical patterns are the easiest to absorb at a first hearing. Traditional forms are easier to recognise as poems than free verse.

Above all, remember that the audience is granted just one chance to appreciate your poem. If it is spoken out slowly and loudly and conveys a clear message it is likely to hold some appeal for everyone who hears it.

Exercises

1   Write a poem in any form based on a colour.
2   Select any six words at random, e.g. by sticking a pin in a dictionary. Write them down in various orders. Does any pattern suggest a poem to you? Is there a surreal poem to be found in juxtaposing your word lists, with a little alteration?
3   Write a list of the next ten poems you intend to produce, and make the briefest of notes for each.

EXTENDING THE SCHEDULE

It is a good idea to set yourself further tasks, creating additional poetry days which feature a balance of interests. You will, of course, emphasise your own special interests within these schedules.

Make notes of your new thoughts for poetry days whenever you can. Then on each writing day you will have a rich source of material to start you off, rather than having to use your creative energy to come up with new ideas.

Make lists of exercises which you think would be valuable and stimulating, and adapt the exercises in this book to give you as many variations as possible.

May your poetry bring you continued joy.

INDEX

ALLISON & BUSBY WRITERS' GUIDES

How to Write **Advertising Features**   £7.99
John Paxton Sheriff

The Craft of Writing **Articles**   £8.99
Gordon Wells

How to Write a **Blockbuster**   £7.99
Sarah Harrison

The **Book Writer's Handbook** 1995/6   £8.99
Gordon Wells

How to Write for **Children**   £8.99
Tessa Krailing

How to Write **Crime Novels**   £6.99
Isobel Lambot

How to Compile and Sell **Crosswords and**   £8.99
Other Puzzles
Graham R Stevenson

How to Write **Five-Minute Features**   £8.99
Alison Chisholm

How to Create **Fictional Characters**   £6.99
Jean Saunders

The Craft of **Food and Cookery Writing**   £7.99
Janet Laurence

How to Write **Historical Novels**   £5.99
Michael Legat